REVISED EDITIO

USEFUL BOOK

Songs and ideas from Play School

ZZZOOOOM
ZZOOOOOOM

REVISED EDITION

USEFUL BOOK

Songs and ideas from Play School

CONTENTS

ABOUT THIS BOOK

In the life of a young child learning, doing, playing, singing are not separate activities. They are integrated. We've tried to reflect this in the planning of a book for people who care for young children.

The songs we have chosen have mostly been 'useful' songs rather than songs for their own sake – songs that are part of everyday life, songs to sing while driving in the car, when feeling hungry, while cleaning the house. Many of them are traditional, or have been published in various books, but many were written especially for our programs. A large number of the songs can be found on the records 'Hey Diddle Diddle', 'Hickory Dickory', 'Humpty Dumpty', and 'Wiggerly Woo'. Our *Play School* pianist, Warren Carr, has placed the melodies within a range which in our experience suits the young child's voice and for which the accompanying guitar chords are simple.

The activities in the book are designed for children from babyhood until early school age. They are grouped by themes rather than by their suitability for a particular age, and can be selected according to the child's level.

The Child Safety Centre at the Royal Alexandra Hospital for Children, Camperdown, Sydney, has provided us with the safety hints included in this book, and members of the hospital's staff have helped us on aspects of child and parent relationships. We have drawn on expert advice for our discussions of aspects of child development, and we owe a debt to the Australian Early Childhood Association's *Today's Child* leaflets.

However, a great number of the ideas in *The Useful Book* have come from parents. It is to parents and to those others who work with and for children that we dedicate this book. We hope that they will find it a source of information and ideas, a 'vocabulary' for playing and a stimulus to have fun with a child.

Henrietta Clark
Early Childhood Unit
ABC

ABOUT THE PROGRAMS

Television

Play School is shown nationally on ABC television twice a day, once in the morning, and a different program in the afternoon. It is made primarily for the pre-school child at home, and is viewed widely in kindergarten classes in infants' schools.

The many regular features of *Play School* such as the familiar presenters, the toys and pets, the windows, the clock and the calendar, provide a dependable, secure base on which the child can build new experiences.

Each week of programs works through a theme, such as Air, Horses or Shapes, and each day emphasises a different strand of the pre-school child's interests.

Monday is Useful Box Day, when we make things out of household bits and pieces. The emphasis is on manual dexterity and creativity.

Tuesday Dressing Up Day, is designed to encourage creative role play. Again, readily available household items are used.

Wednesday is Pets' Day, when we care for the regular pets and extend awareness of other animals.

Thursday Imagination Day, puts emphasis on imaginative play.

Friday Science Day, contains a simple experiment, extending knowledge about the week's theme. Among other things, it seeks to encourage the child's curiosity and wonder about the world.

On each day there is a story (introduced by a look at the clock) and a film (introduced through the windows). There are songs to sing, and music for movement. The band of presenters is large enough to provide variety (two, a man and a woman, present each program) but small enough for each to become a known friend.

In *Play School,* everything is for the child. The things to make and do, the humour, the language and the music are all adapted to the appropriate level and everything is presented directly *to* the child. The presenters do not speak to other children in the studio; they speak straight to the viewing child — one child, not children *en masse*. The child is encouraged to respond spontaneously, offering opinions, answering questions and participating in activities.

Play School is essentially a realistic program; the presenters are natural, and real things happen. Puppets are seen to be puppets, and gingerbread men take twenty minutes to make. An attempt is made to help a child distinguish between reality and fantasy, and to provide an introduction to the extraordinary medium of television at the relevant level of understanding.

Radio

Children Today, a program for parents and children, is broadcast each morning Monday to Friday.

Children Today—

. . . looks at children's growth and development; at their physical well-being; at the inner world of their intellect and imagination and the outer world of their relationships with adults and other children

. . . provides an opportunity to hear the experiences and opinions of people involved in child-rearing and caring as well as tapping the knowledge and observations of specialists in early childhood development and other related fields

. . . provides up-to-date information on a range of resources and services for children and caregivers

. . . provides practical suggestions for children's activities.

Children Today also presents songs, stories and poems for young children.

DAY AND NIGHT

The Animals Wake Up

Other animals could wake up too.

A sheep	Baa-aa
A hen	Cluck cluck
A duck	Quack quack
A dog	Bow wow
A cat	Miaow

Hey! Good Morning, Ho! Good Morning

Hey! good morning, Ho! good morning
Sing a morning song,
Hey! good morning, Ho! good morning
Come and sing along.
Hey! good morning, Ho! good morning
Singing can be fun,
Hey! good morning, Ho! good morning
Sing with everyone.

Shadows

On a sunny day, a child can draw around a shadow — in the morning . . . at noon . . . in the evening. See the different things shadows do.

You can make shadows at night, with a light.

Clocks

A clock can be made with a circle of cardboard (a paper plate) a paper fastener, and something for the hands — gum leaves are interesting.

Turn the hands to the next high point of the day and put the clock next to a real clock. When the hands of both clocks are in the same position — the time has come!

Young children have little concept of time. Rather than talking about hours and minutes, refer to punctuation points in the child's day, e.g., 'after Ben goes to school' or 'after lunch.' For short time periods, try an egg-timer or a kitchen timer.

Going to Sleep

Sometimes children are afraid of going to sleep. They may fear being abandoned, or they may fear the dark, even though they *know* there's nothing to hurt them. Such fears are very real to a child.

Security may come with:

- An easing of the separation. Take time to settle the child in bed, perhaps with a story, rhyme or song.
- An open door through which the sounds of the household may be heard — people moving about, the radio or TV playing softly.
- A night-light.
- A special toy to cuddle, chosen by the child.
- Making friends with the night, and saying, 'Goodnight moon, goodnight street light, goodnight stars'.

All fabrics will burn, but some burn more readily than others. So see that the night clothes you buy your children are either: Made from fabrics which are slow to burn, or designed to reduce the risk of their catching alight.

Dingle Dangle Scarecrow

When all the hens were roosting, and the moon behind a cloud,
Up jumped the scarecrow, and shouted very loud:
'I'm a dingle dangle scarecrow', *etc*

This Little Boy

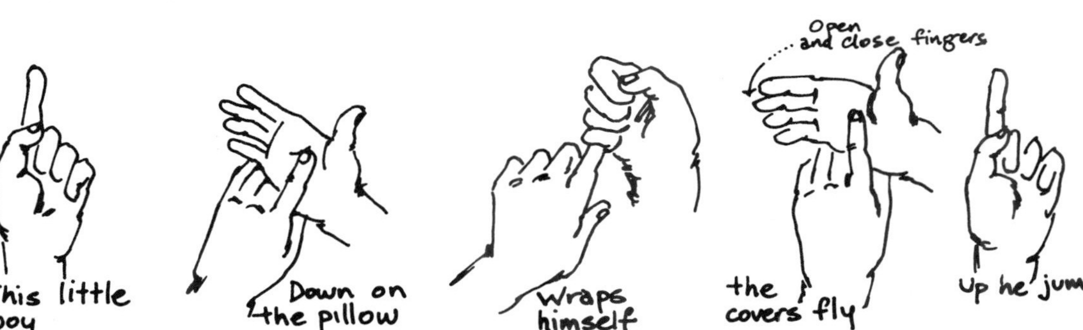

RAIN AND WIND

Rain Song

G D G G D G
Rain is fall - ing down. Rain is fall - ing down.
G D G D G D G
Pit - ter pat - ter pit - ter pat - ter Rain is fall - ing down.

It's Raining

C C C C C
It's rain - ing, it's pour - ing, The old man is snor - ing.
C C C C
Went to bed and he bumped his head, And he did-n't get up in the morn - ing.

Going Out

It's fun on a wet day to go out, at least for a while.

- Watch the clouds. Can you tell when it will rain . . . when it will stop?
- Sail leaves down the gutters.
- Watch the course the water takes as it runs downhill.
- Watch raindrops splashing in puddles, or if the rain has stopped, help find your child's reflection in a puddle.
- As the sun comes out, stand with your back to it and look at the sky. Is there a rainbow? Notice how different everything smells after rain, even in the city.

Playing Inside

Some children have almost too many toys. You could keep some aside, and bring them out on a wet day, or you could have some toys that are only played with on wet days. Or make up a wet day treasure bag with surprise oddments.

If children are cooped up inside all day, they will need to let off steam. They could:

- Make cubby houses with the furniture and some old sheets and blankets.
- Put on a record or tape, and dance.
- Make a ball out of an old pair of panty hose. Turn them inside out so that the legs go inside the waist part. Stuff them with old newspaper and tie them securely. The ball can be thrown vigorously and should not cause too much damage.

Quieter occupations could include:

- Cooking (see recipes p. 38)
- Painting in a slightly more elaborate way than usual, e.g. printing with vegetables, putting up a *big* piece of paper on the bathroom wall and painting a mural, painting on windows or mirrors.
- Making jewellery, e.g., a macaroni necklace, painted, a milk bottle top brooch or a bracelet of cut-up plastic straws. This might start a dress-up activity.

Thunder

I Hear Thunder

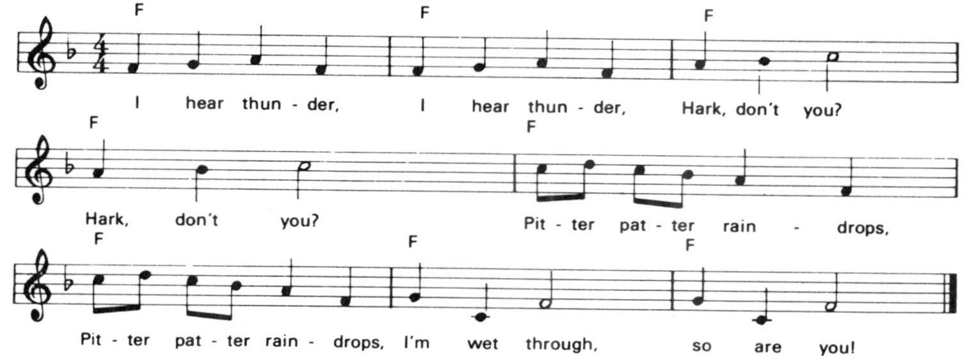

Anything sudden or unexpected can frighten a young child, who may well be scared by thunder. Perhaps this is a time to accept the child's fear, to give comfort and to allow the child into your bed.

- When the child is confident, you could play thunder games. Watch for lightning, then count slowly until you hear the thunder. You have counted about how many kilometres away the storm is.
- Make thunder noises. Stamp around noisily or find a big piece of cardboard to use as a wobbly thunder board. You could also rattle dried peas, pebbles or pasta on an old tin tray, or shake rice or little stones in a plastic bottle to make the sound of the rain.

Be sure a child is dressed to be clearly visible in wet weather or at night. Never double park near a school or kindergarten and always discharge your passengers on the kerb side of the car.

The Wind

Who Has Seen the Wind?

A young child is usually happy to run around with a kite-shaped piece of paper trailing and fluttering on a string, but here is a pattern for a kite that should fly.

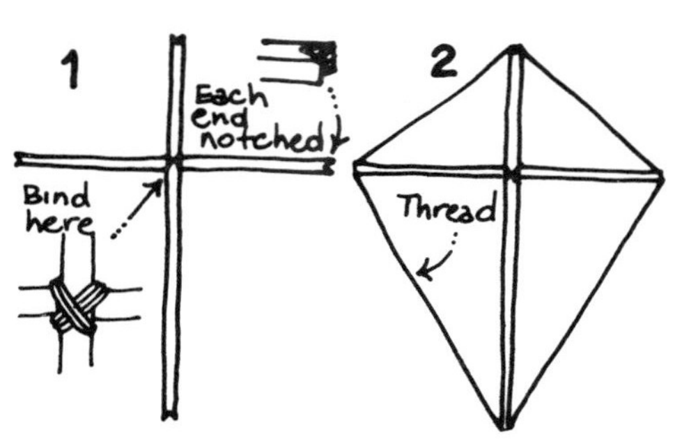

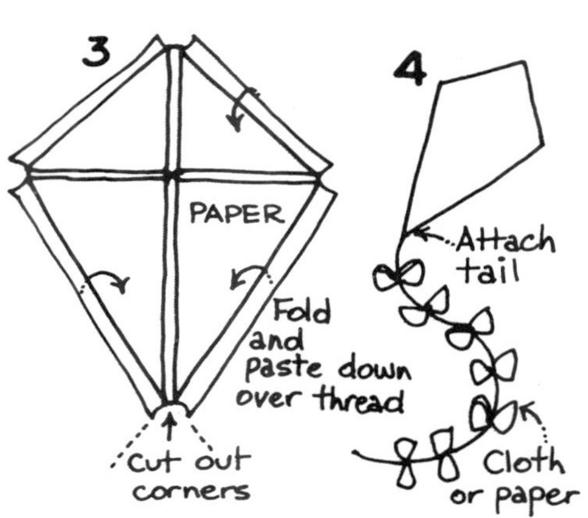

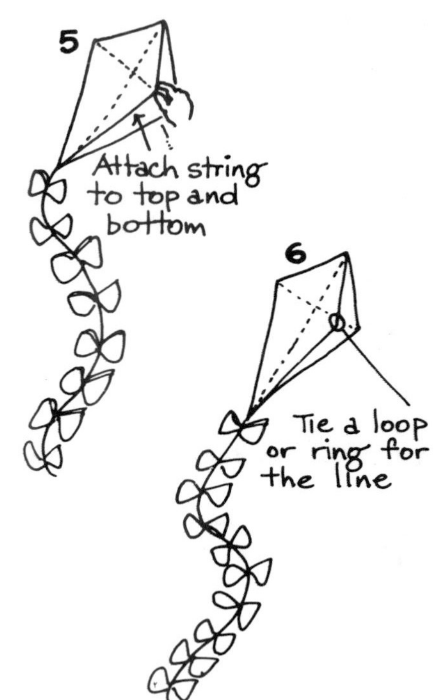

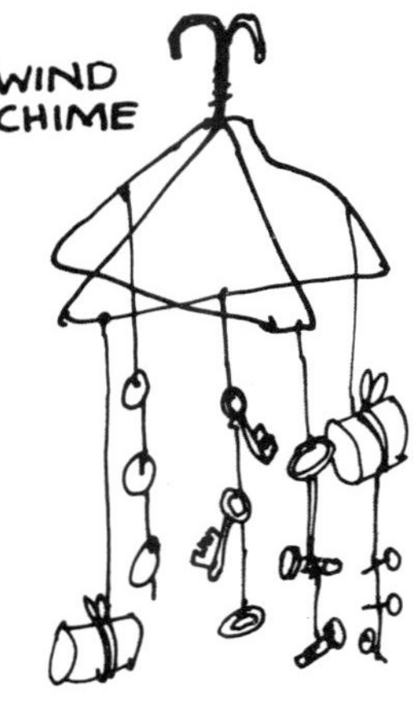

How do you know the wind is passing by?

- Draw your child's attention to the feel of the wind on the hair and skin by licking an arm and holding it up in the wind to feel the sensation.
- Watch flags flying, trees bending, the washing flapping on the line. Try to catch a falling leaf. Hold some paper streamers up in the wind – are they blowing the same way as the trees?
- Listen to the sounds of blowing leaves, rattling windows, the wind moaning through cracks. Make a wind chime to hang up.

Children can be very responsive to weather conditions. Wind, for example, can have the most extraordinary effect on them. They can become irritable, over-excited and unsettled.

FIRST GAMES

Young children learn about themselves by trying things out, by seeing what they can do, seeing what they can cause to happen, and by seeing how other people react to them.

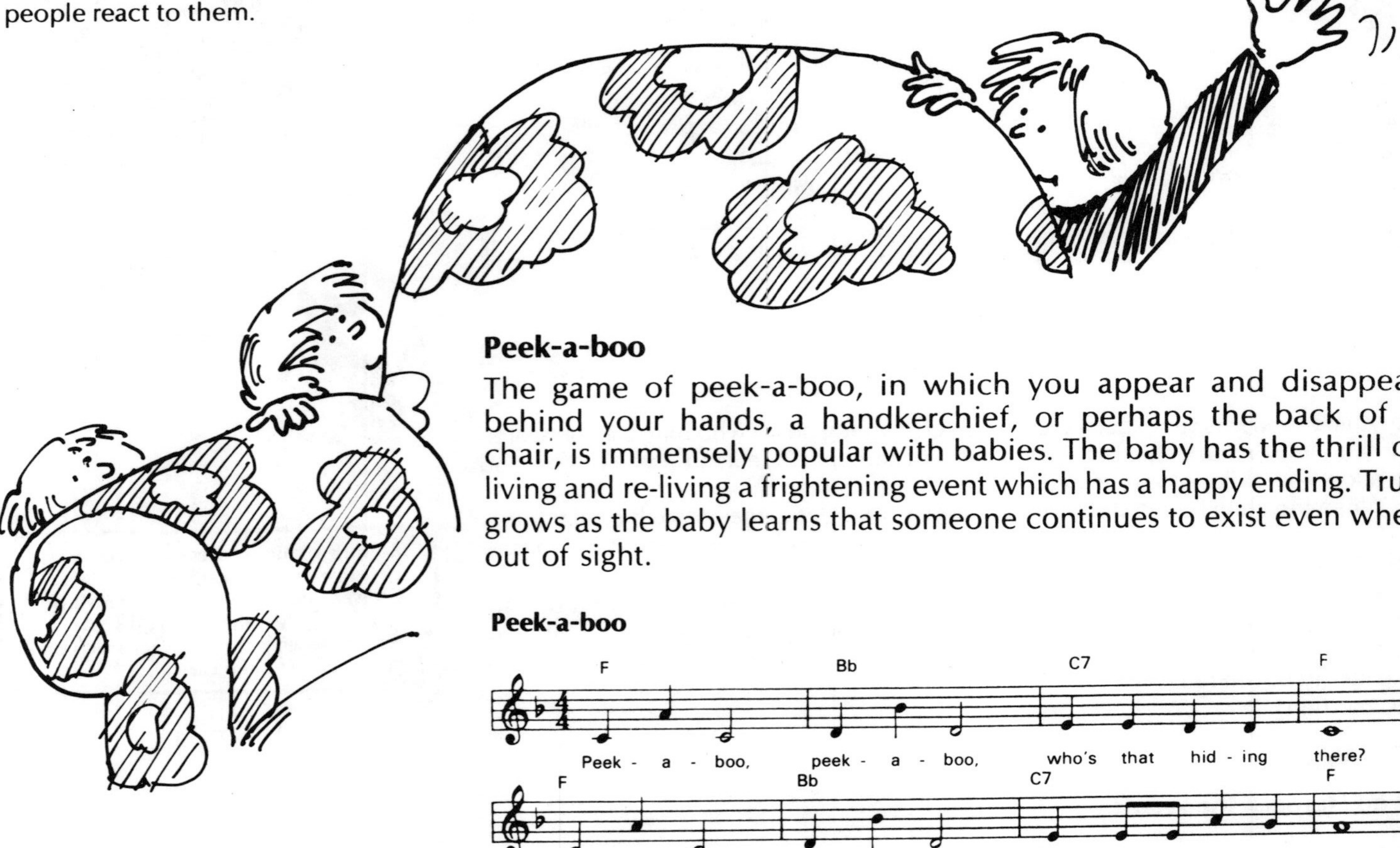

Peek-a-boo

The game of peek-a-boo, in which you appear and disappear behind your hands, a handkerchief, or perhaps the back of a chair, is immensely popular with babies. The baby has the thrill of living and re-living a frightening event which has a happy ending. Trust grows as the baby learns that someone continues to exist even when out of sight.

Peek-a-boo

F Bb C7 F
Peek - a - boo, peek - a - boo, who's that hid - ing there?
F Bb C7 F
Peek - a - boo, Peek - a - boo, (Pet - er's) be - hind the chair.

Jack in the Box

C C C F
Jack is qui - et down in his box Un - til
Fm Fm C
some - one o - pens the lid. Boo!

As they grow, children gradually come to understand that they have an identity, that they are of a certain sex, that he or she has a name that means him or her. Their names are very important to them.

Oh, What Do You Think My Name Is?

C C G7
Oh, what do you think my name is? I won - der if you
C F C
know, My name is .... Hel-
G7 C G7 C
- lo, hel - lo, hel - lo hel - lo, Hel - lo, hel - lo, hel - lo.

An important part of learning who one is, is learning about one's own body. A lot of children's games and activities foster this self-awareness.

This Little Pig

This little pig went to market,
This little pig stayed home,
This little pig had roast beef,
This little pig had none,
This little pig cried
Wee, wee, wee, all the way home.

Round and Round the Garden

Round and round the garden,
Like a teddy bear,
One step, two step,
Tickly under there!

There Was a Little Mouse

There was a little mouse,
And he lived just . . . here,
And every time you touched him,
He ran right up . . . here!

Heads and Shoulders, Knees and Toes

Eyes and ears and mouth and nose
Mouth and nose, mouth and nose
Eyes and ears and mouth and nose
We all clap hands together.

Touch each part of the body as it is mentioned.
(This song is often sung to the melody of 'There is a Tavern in the Town'.)

Some Body Activities

- Lay the child down on some newspapers stuck together. Draw an outline right round the child. Then have fun painting it, sticking scraps of material on for clothes, or dressing the figure up in something outlandish.
- Mix up some paint and try handprints and footprints, thumbprints and toe-prints. Make them into patterns.
- Do you have a mirror that a child can see a full-length reflection in?
- Have you measured your child's height? Use the inside of a cupboard door. You could mark off the height with a line, write name and date, and show the child the difference next time you measure.
- Do you take photographs? Children like to see the stages they have passed through.

Put Your Finger on Your Nose

Put your finger on your eyes,
They make a good disguise.

Put your finger on your cheek,
Leave it there about a week.

Put your finger on your ear,
Leave it there about a year.

GAMES WITH HANDS

Clap Your Hands

Finger and hand puppets

You can make finger puppets for yourself and use them to sing a song or tell a story, or make some for a child to use. Draw a small face or animal head (or cut one from a magazine), staple it to a strip of light cardboard, and paste the strip into a circle to fit your finger.

Faces on the fingers of gloves are easy to manipulate. You can draw or stick faces on rubber gloves; embroider little faces on the fingers of a child's gloves, complete with woolly hair; or just draw on the child's fingertips.

A quick hand puppet may be made by laying a large handkerchief over the fingers and pushing the index and middle fingers into a cut-down cardboard cylinder with a face drawn on. Move the other fingers about as arms.

Open, Shut Them

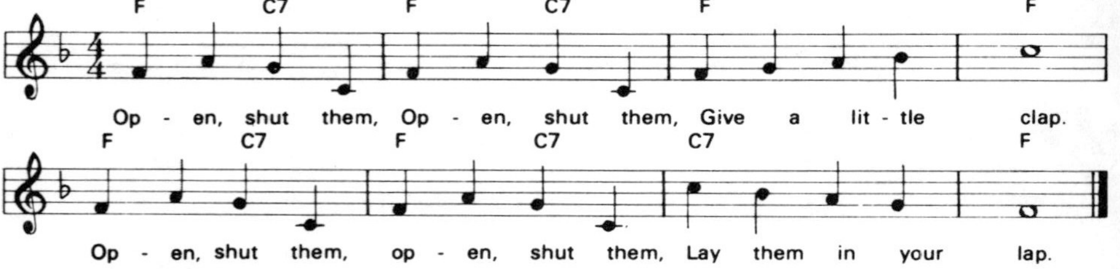

Creep them, creep them, creep them,
Right up to your chin,
Open wide your little mouth,
But do not pop them in.

Falling, falling, falling, falling
Almost to the ground
Quickly raise them up again
And roll them round and round.

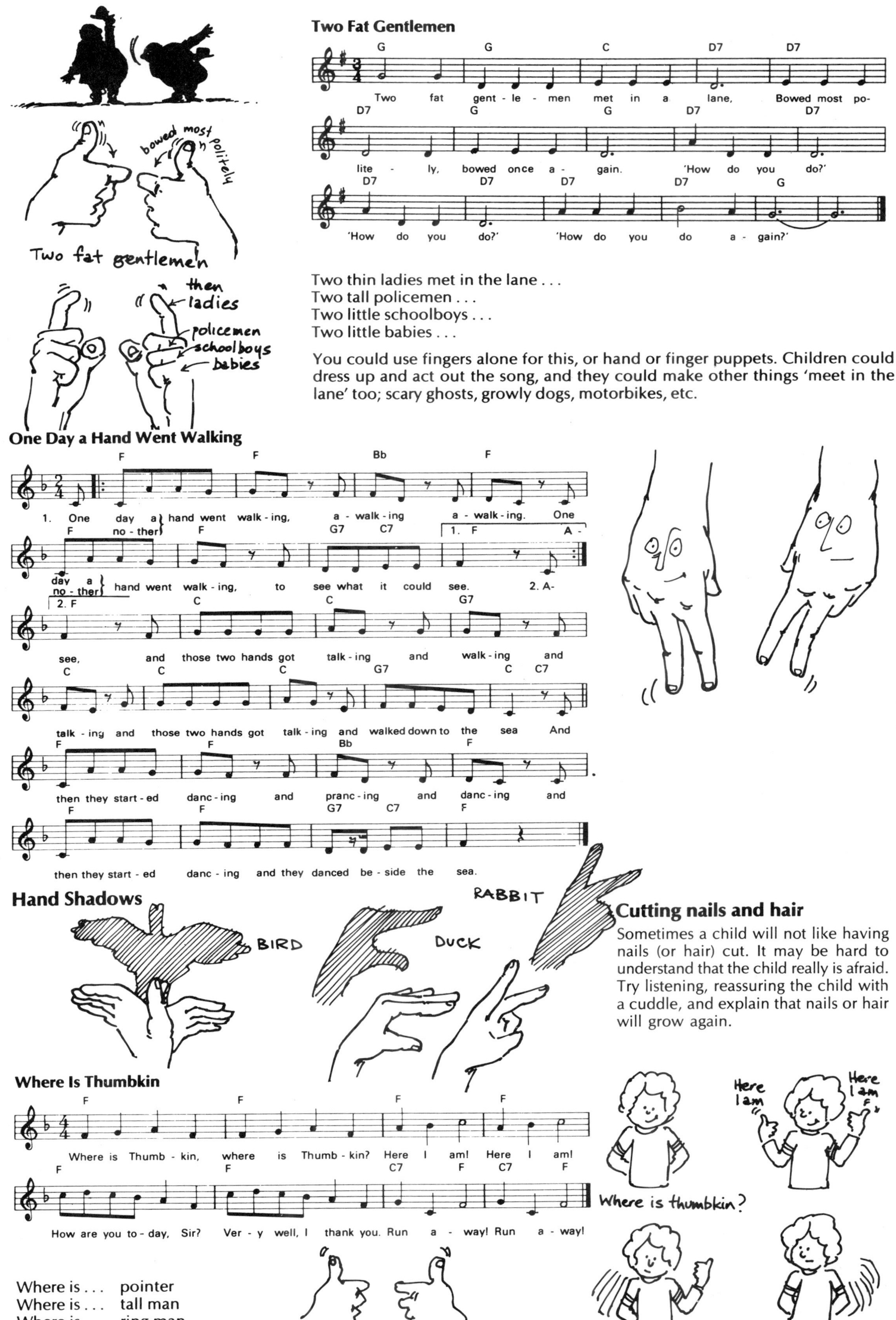

Two thin ladies met in the lane . . .
Two tall policemen . . .
Two little schoolboys . . .
Two little babies . . .

You could use fingers alone for this, or hand or finger puppets. Children could dress up and act out the song, and they could make other things 'meet in the lane' too; scary ghosts, growly dogs, motorbikes, etc.

Cutting nails and hair

Sometimes a child will not like having nails (or hair) cut. It may be hard to understand that the child really is afraid. Try listening, reassuring the child with a cuddle, and explain that nails or hair will grow again.

Where is . . . pointer
Where is . . . tall man
Where is . . . ring man
Where is . . . small man

NURSERY RHYMES

The more that is learned about child development, the more we come to understand the importance of early communication between parent and child. A parent who talks to a baby, sings or recites nursery rhymes, even before the baby can understand a word, is helping the baby to understand that language is a process of communication. Some old nursery rhymes may appear meaningless or obscure, sexist, violent or irrelevant, but with their simple melodies, basic rhythms and bizarre images, they have a permanent place in the lore of parents and children.

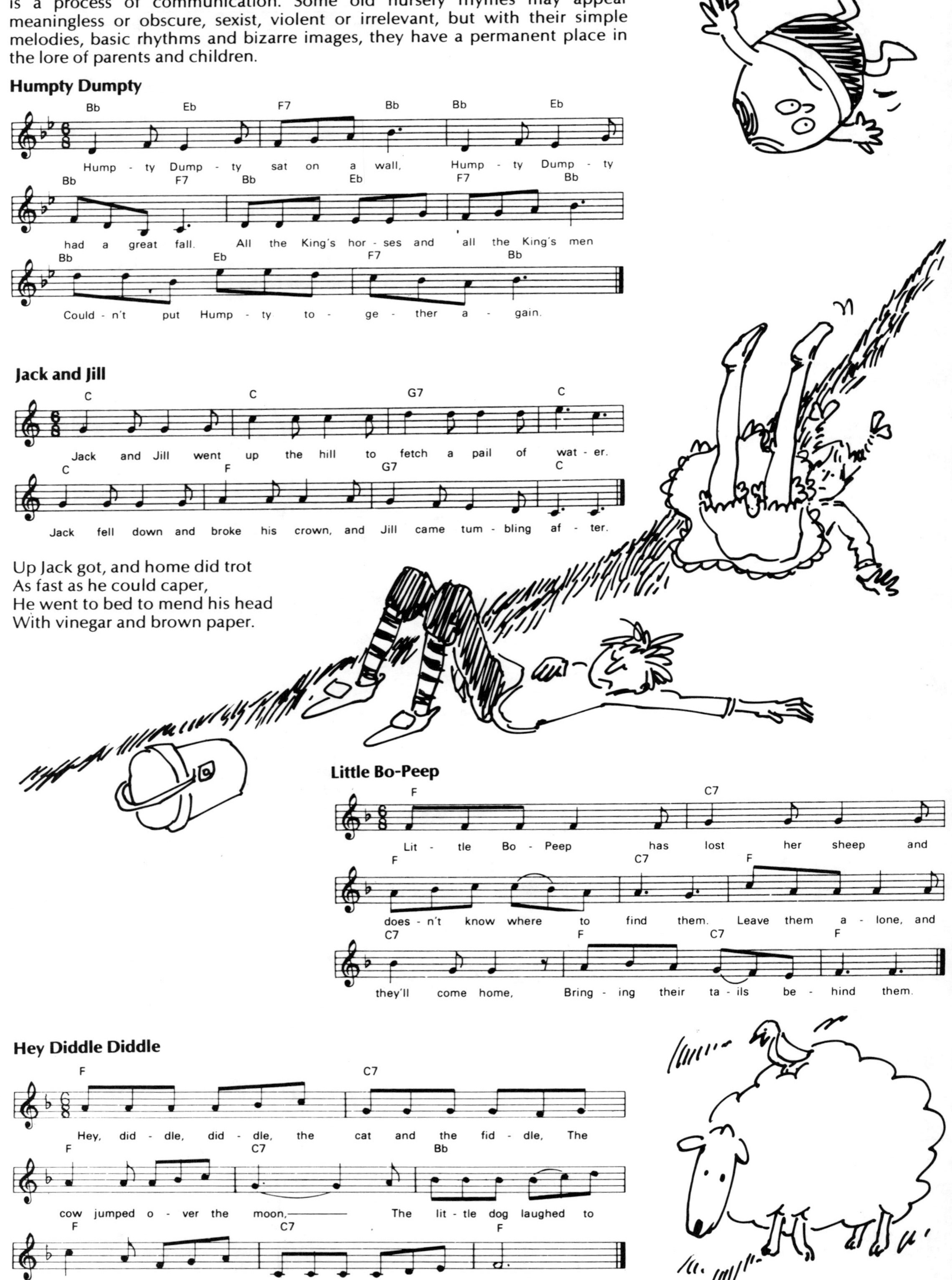

Up Jack got, and home did trot
As fast as he could caper,
He went to bed to mend his head
With vinegar and brown paper.

Sing a Song of Sixpence

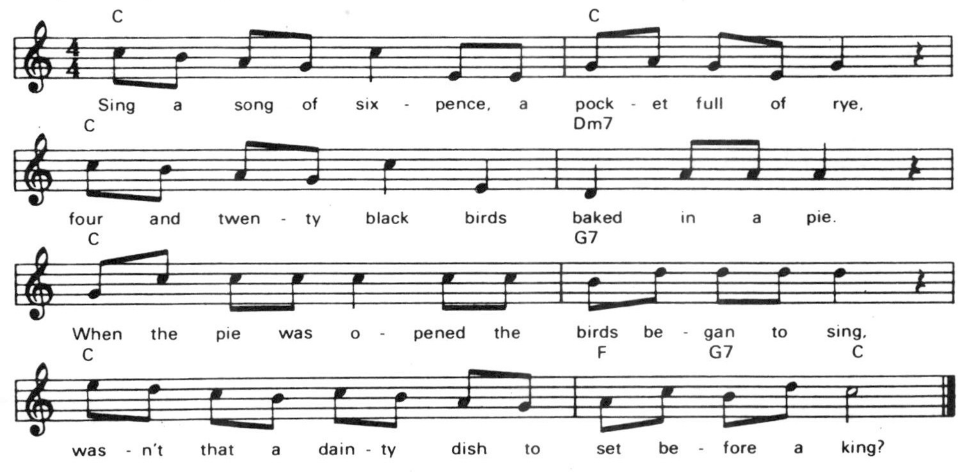

The king was in his counting house
Counting out his money,
The queen was in the parlour, eating bread and honey,
The maid was in the garden, hanging out the clothes,
When down came a blackbird, and pecked off her nose.

Three Blind Mice

Baa Baa Black Sheep

Hickory Dickory Dock

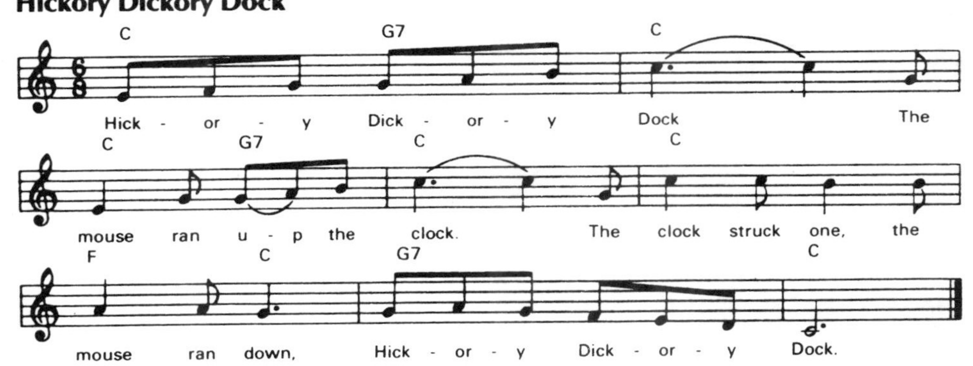

Three mice to make

A surprise mouse can hide in a matchbox. Boo!

You can make a mouse out of a cotton wool ball. Twist up the ears and stick on a string tail.

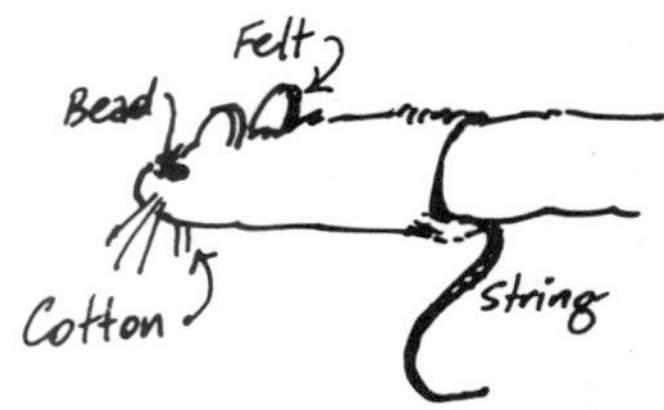

A 'finger' mouse to fit a child's finger can be made by sewing a piece of furry fabric into a cone shape. Add felt ears and a string tail. A less permanent mouse can be made of cardboard.

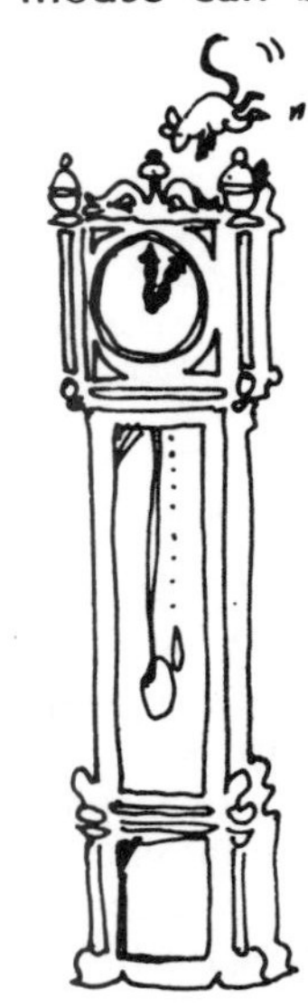

CHILDREN'S TOYS

Through playing, a young child learns. For a child, play is not a relaxation from work, as it is for adults. It is the most important activity.

Many of the ideas in this book show you how to help your child play and learn, without your having to buy anything; however, for the city child who cannot wander into the natural environment to find playthings, commercial toys are important.

When choosing a toy, think about the child's age and personality, what he or she likes doing now or, perhaps, is just on the verge of doing. Belonging to a toy library is an excellent way of trying out toys on your child as well as extending the variety of playthings. When buying toys, most good toyshops will help you to choose.

Suggestions for toys

For a very *small* baby just learning to use the senses:

- A mobile to look at.
- A hand toy that feels nice, is easy to grasp and safe to suck.

As the baby *grows older*, the exploration becomes more elaborate:

- A string of beads across the pram or cot to reach out for, or kick at, which will help test distance judgment. (Remove it before sleep.)
- Some toys of different textures to feel.
- One small soft toy to love and cuddle as the baby learns to cope with separation.

For a *crawling* baby who is exploring motion:

- Any sort of toy that rolls or pushes along, especially one that makes an interesting noise.
- A soft cloth ball that rolls but is easy to grasp.

For a *just-walking* baby:

- Anything to push around.
- A baby walker.
- A little bike without pedals to encourage self-propulsion.

Once walking is mastered, the child is exploring a whole new world, keenly practising co-ordination of hand and eye, learning to recognise shapes, working out sizes and relationships.

- Some large wooden blocks (which might be the start of a collection that can grow year by year).
- Some rings on a post.
- A set of plastic cups that stack and nest.
- A hammering toy.

From now until the reading stage the child will continue to use toys that exercise skills in co-ordination, shape recognition, construction, etc. These toys are designed with increasing complexity to suit the child's growing capacity:

- Sand and water equipment, perhaps including a watering can.
- Painting equipment. A set of big bottles of paint and some thick brushes would make good presents, and so would some thick, washable felt-tipped pens.
- Science equipment, a big magnifying glass or a magnet.
- Things to pretend with — little cars, dolls and doll equipment, a toy telephone, a hand puppet, a tea set, a box of sticking plaster.
- Books to suit the child's age.
- Outdoor adventure equipment such as a rope ladder.
- Building equipment — more of those wooden blocks, a construction set.
- Games — picture dominoes, picture snap.
- Equipment to practise matching and fitting. Jigsaws, especially with interesting pieces that can do service in different contexts. Peg board sets.
- Music to listen to, sing, move, play. A good xylophone. A record.

Your child will take many cues from you, so if you denigrate some toys, the child may not care for them either.

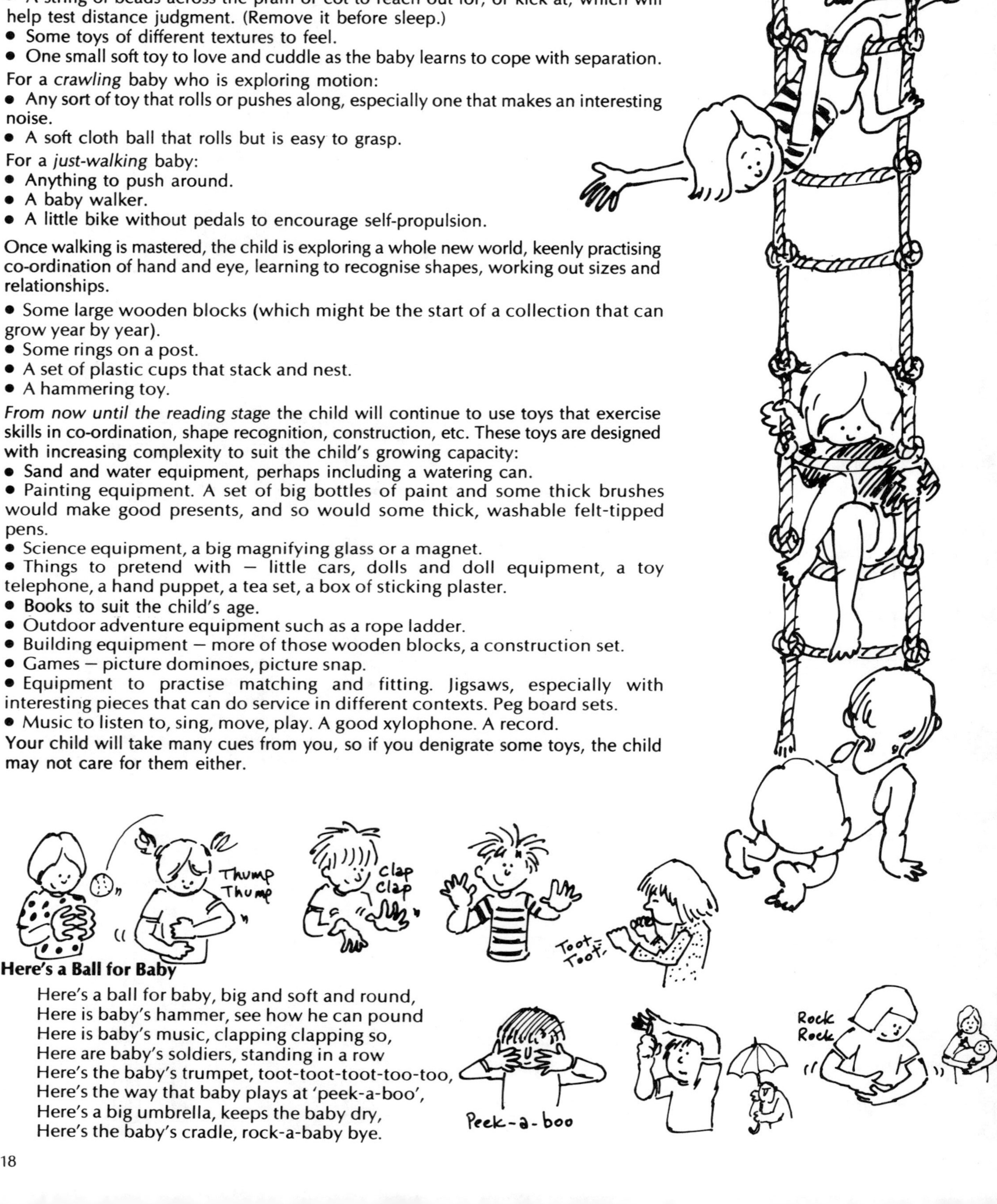

Here's a Ball for Baby

Here's a ball for baby, big and soft and round,
Here is baby's hammer, see how he can pound
Here is baby's music, clapping clapping so,
Here are baby's soldiers, standing in a row
Here's the baby's trumpet, toot-toot-toot-too-too,
Here's the way that baby plays at 'peek-a-boo',
Here's a big umbrella, keeps the baby dry,
Here's the baby's cradle, rock-a-baby bye.

PARTIES

To a young child a birthday is an indication of being a very special individual, loved by the whole family. It is exciting proof, too, of growing up and one day getting to be a 'four' or a 'big five'.

Five Little Candles

Four little candles . . . three . . . two, etc.
One little candle straight and tall,
Only one is left, that's all,
Pouf! I blow with all my might,
And out goes that little candle light.

Watch a candle flame for a while. See how it flickers and changes shape.

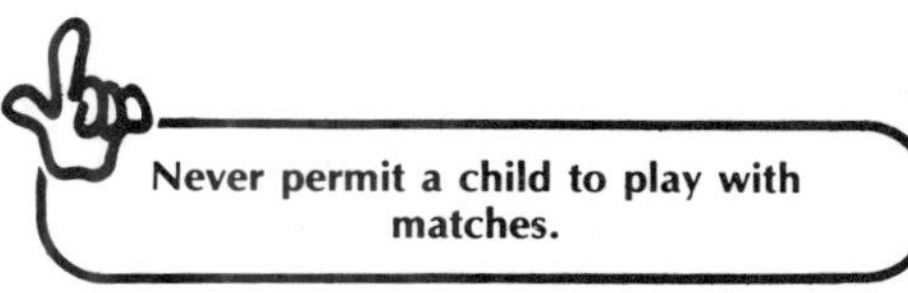

Things to make for a party

cut out this piece
LIGHT CARDBOARD
Staple
Susan
Crepe paper fringing
Elastic
PARTY HATS
cut here

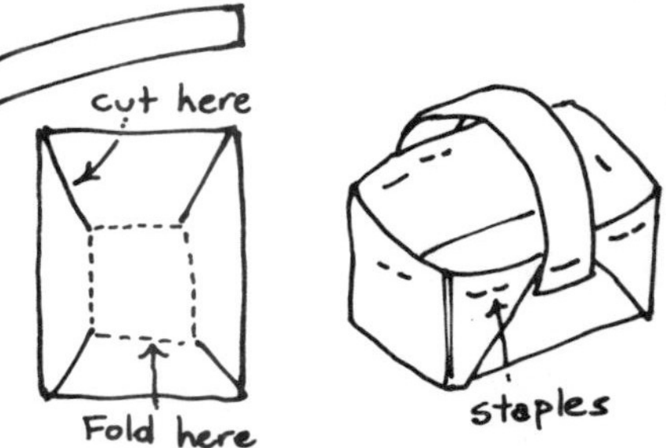

A BASKET TO TAKE THINGS HOME IN

Managing a party

- Involve your child in the preparations, but don't build up expectations to the point of over-excitement. It could easily end in tears.
- Plan the party with suitable activities but don't be rigid. Two- and three-year-olds aren't ready for organised games.
- Some children, including your own, may not want to join in. Don't force them because you have a preconceived idea of the 'party'.
- Have a quiet activity before the meal, and sit down to eat.
- Another adult is a great help, especially when people are arriving and departing.
- When the presents are opened, make sure each donor is thanked and each present treated with respect.
- Handing out something to take home is one way of ensuring each guest has your attention at good-bye time.

The children are learning about how to behave at a party, and you, by behaving as a host, will help their learning.

FUNNY BALLOONS

Happy Birthday

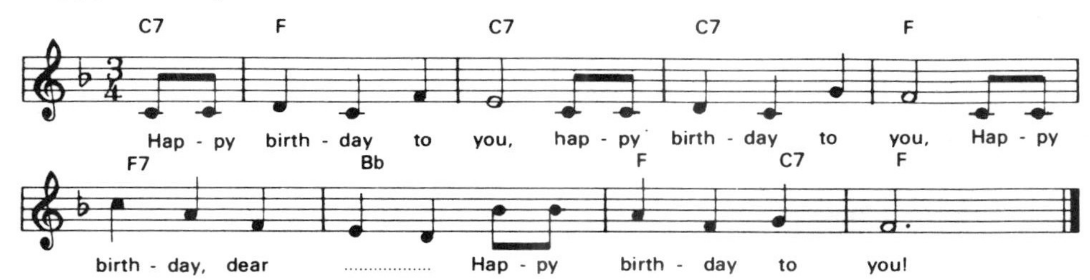

Presents

- Try to discourage people from giving your child sweets as presents or rewards.
- When giving a present, use the same criteria you would use in choosing a toy for your own child — the age and what he or she likes doing.
- Presents need not be expensive. The less expensive items of 'equipment' (e.g., coloured cardboard, a watering can, a magnet) can give great pleasure.

Never give nuts to a child under five. They can be dangerous if inhaled and may result in a trip to hospital. Watch for the child who goes round drinking dregs from glasses, or to whom a thoughtless adult may give alcohol.

HUMPTY Pattern to make

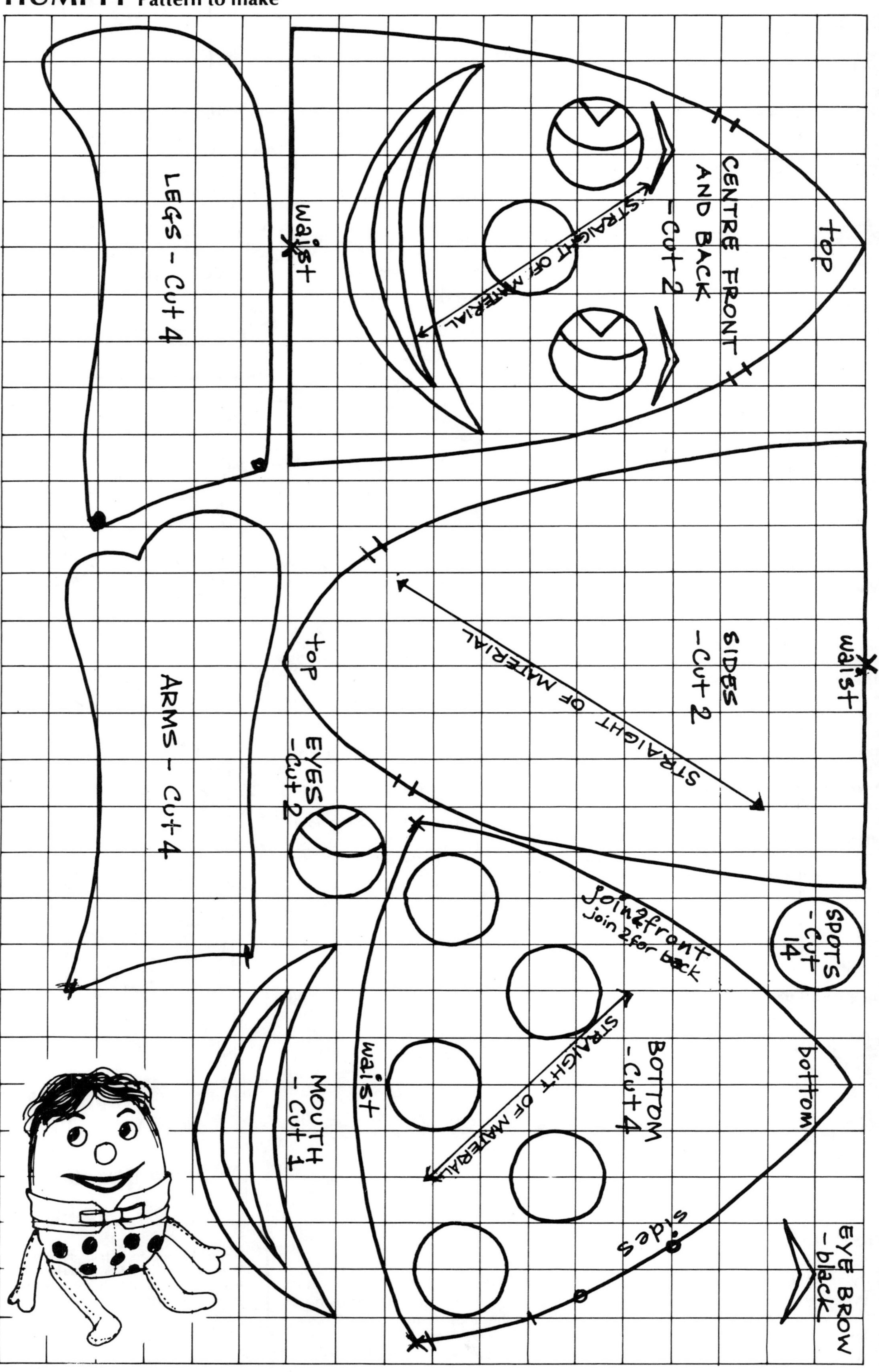

JEMIMA Pattern to make

JEMIMA
SCALE 1cm = 2cm
½cm seams allowed on patterns.

1. Join side back head and attach to face.
2. Seam body leave neck open.
3. Fill head and body separately. Join head to body by hand.
4. Cut feet from black felt. Join to leg and fill.
5. Make arms and fill.
6. Join arms and legs to body by hand.
7. Cut 32cm lengths of wool.
8. Sew a length of tape down centre of wool and attach to centre back seam of head.
9. Embroider mouth, stick on felt cheeks and eyes.

HUMPTY DUMPTY
SCALE 1cm = 2cm
½cm seams allowed on patterns.

1. Top. Join sides to centre front and centre back.
2. Join 4 bottom sections together.
3. Attach top waist to bottom waist matching seams on bottom to notches on top, leave opening to fill. Bottom section needs to be slightly eased onto top.
4. Seam arms and legs and fill.
5. Attach arms and legs to matching marks on seams by hand.
6. Cut 15 red spots for bottom, 2 white felt eyes with black felt inserts, 1 red felt mouth, two black eyebrows, 1 cotton ball for nose (or make a PomPom).
7. Hair: Black wool tuft attached at top of Head.
8. Collar — could be felt 6cm wide with bow tie or ribbon tied.

STORIES

Storytime is an intimate, sharing experience. Children love to hear stories about themselves. These are very easy to make up, and the child will enjoy helping in the telling.

The most popular published stories in the early years are about common experiences. They help the child to understand and interpret events which occur in everyday life, especially if you break off the reading to link the child to the story. A young child will probably not comprehend a long story which has a thread of cause and effect. Begin with shorter stories that have interesting incidents, stories that make use of rhythms and repetition, stories that are imaginative but not fantastic. If you're not sure, a children's librarian will help.

You don't always have to read the words in a book because you can 'tell' the pictures, but as children grow older they need to understand that the printed word remains permanent and that 'elephant', for example, always says elephant. You're not helping development if you paraphrase and change the story every time.

Let the child turn the pages sometimes to connect the printed words with your speech and to see that you read from left to right and from the top to the bottom of the page. You can record some favourite stories on tape so that the child can listen while looking at the book. Allow time on the tape for turning the pages.

Seeing others enjoy books is likely to make your child feel that books have value.

A story to draw as you tell

Use a washable felt pen. Lay the child's hand on a sheet of paper and start drawing at the wrist. Draw round the fingers, keeping the pen on the paper all the time as you tell a story about you and the child having to go to the supermarket via various landmarks (one for each finger). Adapt the story entirely to your child and your own neighbourhood. Having arrived at the supermarket, you have forgotten your shopping list and return the same way for it. Go back to the supermarket and discover you've forgotten your money. Return for that, and back to the supermarket. (You can make more trips to and fro if the child is enjoying the game). When you eventually finish the shopping, 'Amanda' complains that she's tired, so you say 'All right, we'll fly home', and draw over the child's wrist.

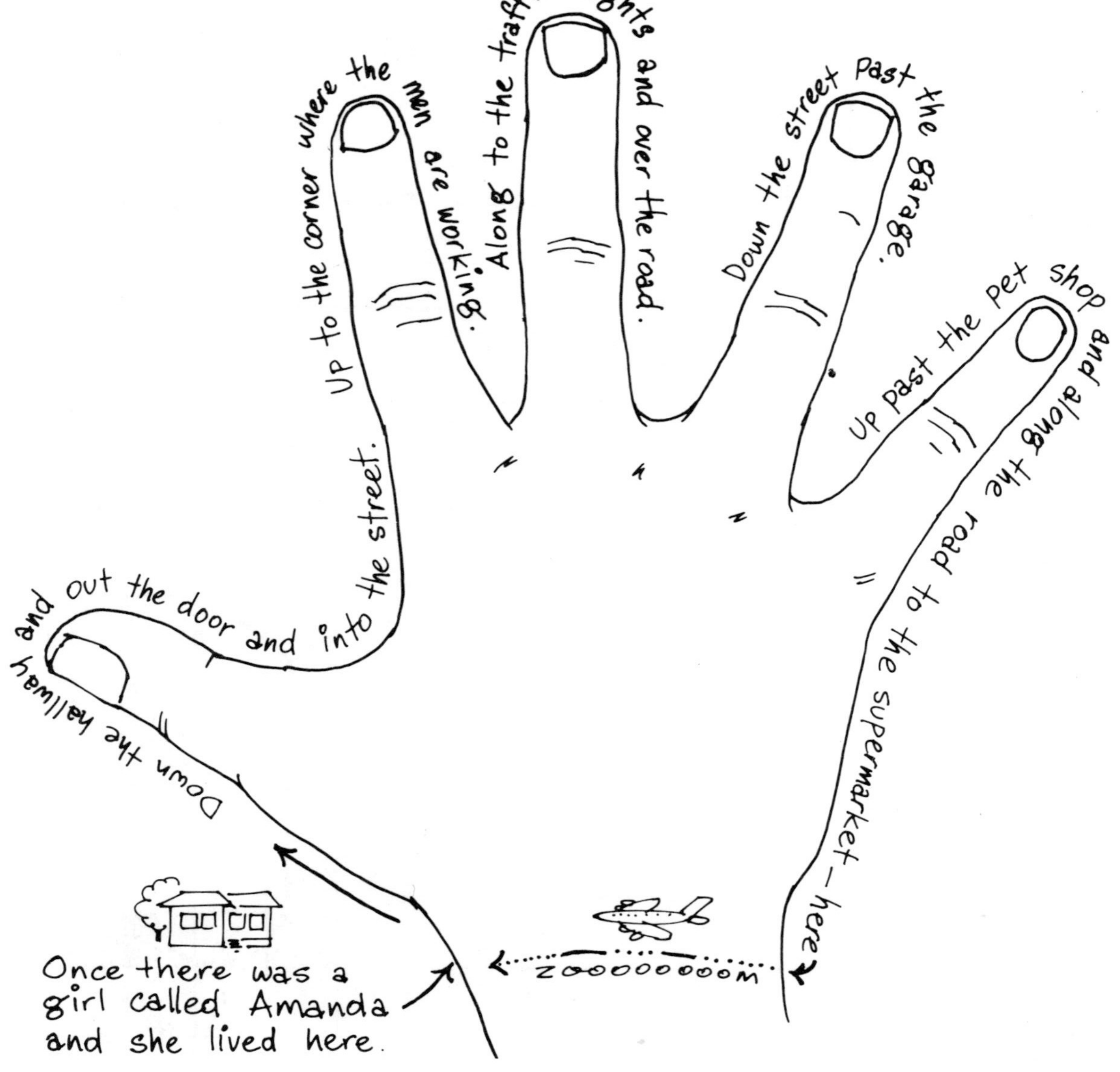

MUSIC

A young child may be frustrated by not knowing the words to express thoughts, feelings and ideas. Maybe music will help express them.

Through music, a child can be given the opportunity:
- To experience rhythm, to discover its flow, progression, balance, its build and climax.
- To move to music.
- To work in harmony with other people, singing together, moving in co-operation.
- To feel happy inside.

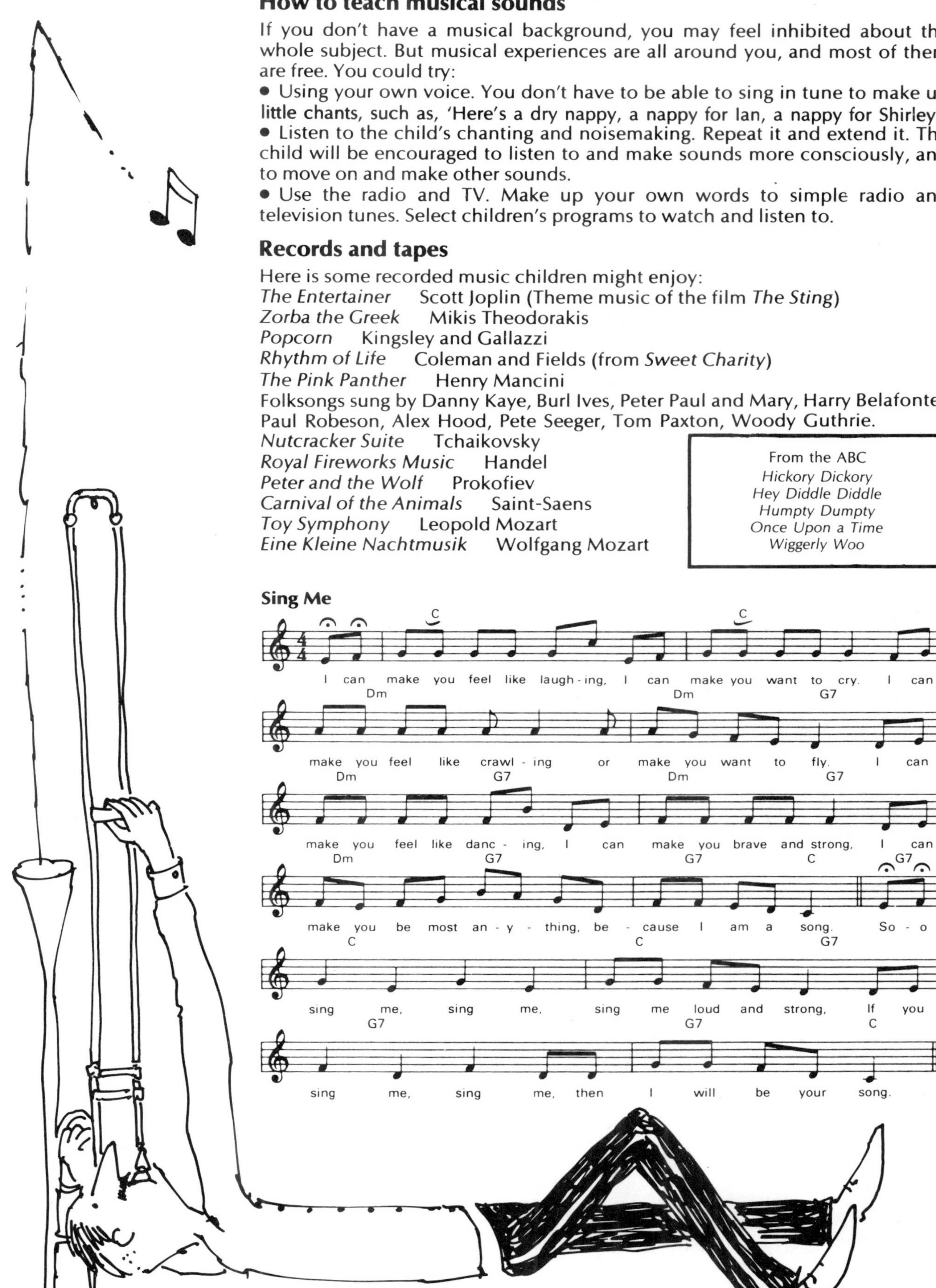

How to teach musical sounds

If you don't have a musical background, you may feel inhibited about the whole subject. But musical experiences are all around you, and most of them are free. You could try:
- Using your own voice. You don't have to be able to sing in tune to make up little chants, such as, 'Here's a dry nappy, a nappy for Ian, a nappy for Shirley'.
- Listen to the child's chanting and noisemaking. Repeat it and extend it. The child will be encouraged to listen to and make sounds more consciously, and to move on and make other sounds.
- Use the radio and TV. Make up your own words to simple radio and television tunes. Select children's programs to watch and listen to.

Records and tapes

Here is some recorded music children might enjoy:
The Entertainer Scott Joplin (Theme music of the film *The Sting*)
Zorba the Greek Mikis Theodorakis
Popcorn Kingsley and Gallazzi
Rhythm of Life Coleman and Fields (from *Sweet Charity*)
The Pink Panther Henry Mancini
Folksongs sung by Danny Kaye, Burl Ives, Peter Paul and Mary, Harry Belafonte, Paul Robeson, Alex Hood, Pete Seeger, Tom Paxton, Woody Guthrie.
Nutcracker Suite Tchaikovsky
Royal Fireworks Music Handel
Peter and the Wolf Prokofiev
Carnival of the Animals Saint-Saens
Toy Symphony Leopold Mozart
Eine Kleine Nachtmusik Wolfgang Mozart

From the ABC
Hickory Dickory
Hey Diddle Diddle
Humpty Dumpty
Once Upon a Time
Wiggerly Woo

Sing Me

MOVING ABOUT

A parent may find it relatively easy to provide a child with materials with which to express and develop creative instincts in art, drama, sculpture or music. But the instinct to move with the whole body, freely and expressively — to dance — is one that some parents find harder to promote at home. (You can feel such a fool twirling round the clothes line when your neighbour looks over the fence.) You could try:

- Providing a clear space for action.
- Showing pleasure as the child tries out new skills.
- Talking about what the child is doing. (Learning and understanding new words — 'forwards', 'backwards', 'heavy', 'light' — help the child to become more self-aware and more precise in movement.)
- Responding creatively to the child's movements yourself.

You could join in; dance away on your own; jump or sing in time with the child (this will help build awareness of rhythm).

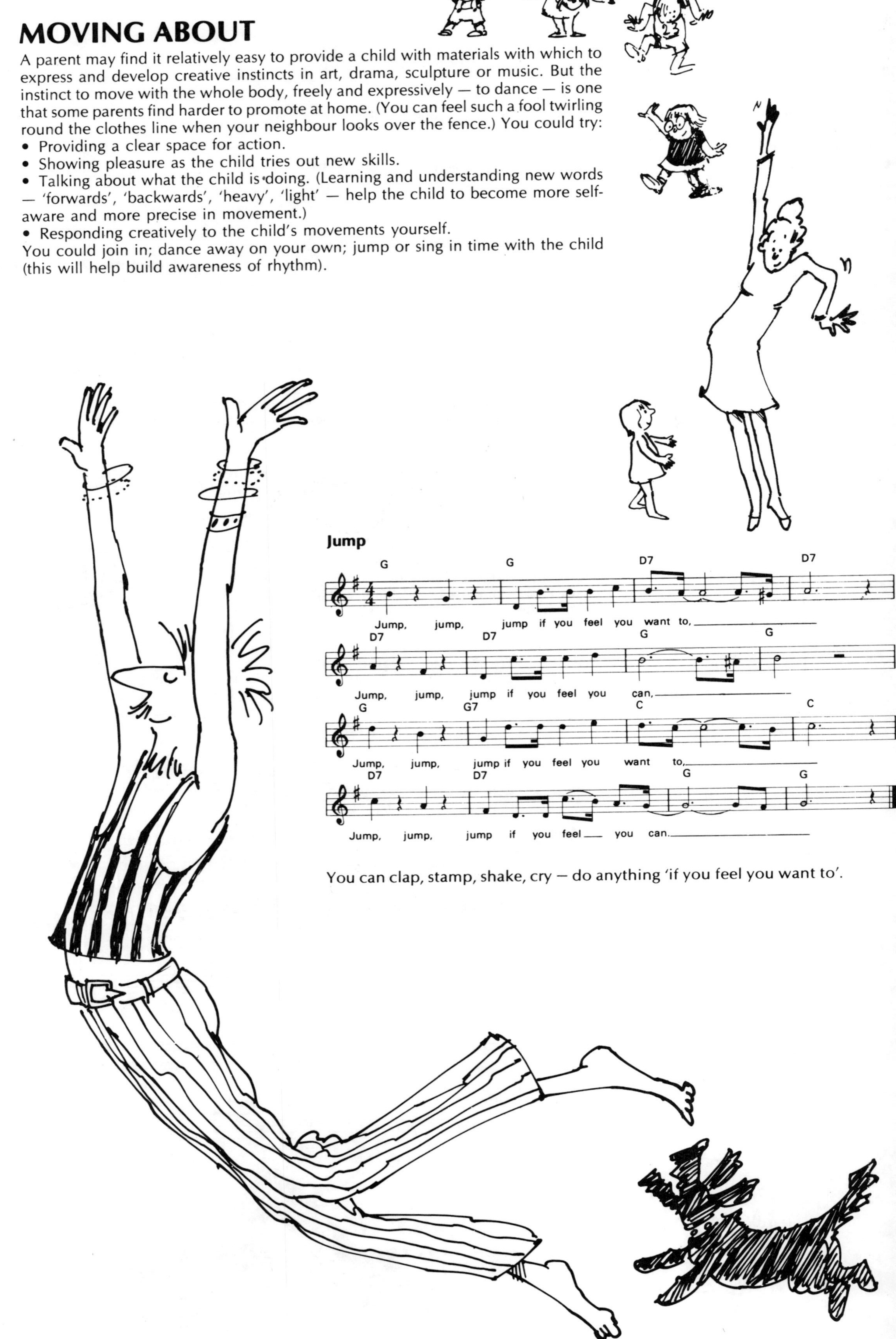

You can clap, stamp, shake, cry — do anything 'if you feel you want to'.

Everybody Do This

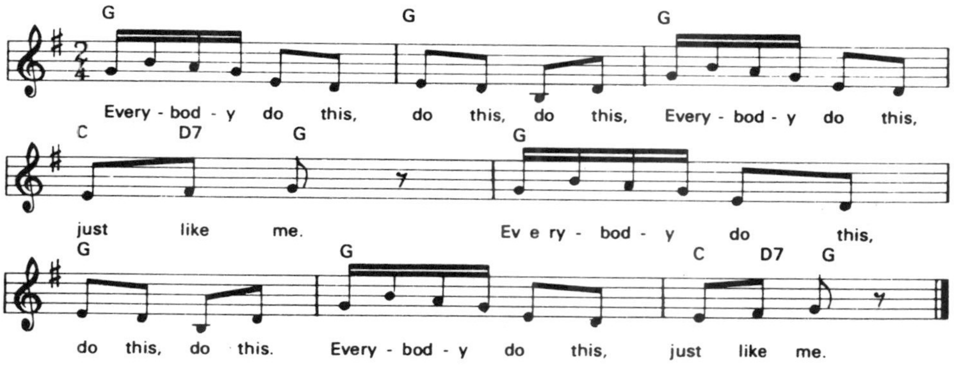

G G G
Every - bod - y do this, do this, do this, Every - bod - y do this,
C D7 G G
just like me. Ev e ry - bod - y do this,
G G C D7 G
do this, do this. Every - bod - y do this, just like me.

Everybody jumping
Everybody running
Everybody clapping
Everybody sleeping, just like me.

What else could everybody do?

I Can Run As Fast As You

F F C7 C7
I can run as fast as you, I can run as fast as you,
F F C7 F
I can run as fast as you, run - ning on the spot.

I can jump as high . . .
I can wobble as much as you . . .

Think of new things to do.

Last verse:

I'm as tired as tired as you
I'm as tired as tired as you
I'm as tired as tired as you
Think I'll have a rest — phew!

Up and Down

F C7 F F
We're go - ing up. we're go - ing up, As high as we can go. We're
Bb F Gm7 F C7 Bb C7
go - ing down, we're go - ing down, We're go - ing way down low,
C7 C7 C7
Up, up, up, up, up, up, up, Down, down, down, down, down.

TALKING AND LISTENING

A child can learn a lot alone, but cannot learn to talk. For that the child needs someone else to listen to, someone to try out words with, someone who talks and listens.

You can help children to develop language ability:

- By talking to them, as babies and as growing children, frequently and lovingly.
- By encouraging their practising of sounds that please them — eg blowing raspberries, babbling etc.
- By helping them to learn new words when they show an interest and by trying to match their actions to the words as they learn them.
- By speaking English (or another language) rather than baby talk.
- By answering their questions simply, factually and with patience.
- By asking questions of them which will require more than one-word answers.
- By extending their phrases and sentences into appropriate grammatical form.
- By offering them a variety of experiences which will stimulate them to talk, including visits to the park, the zoo, the shops etc. and including, of course, the regular reading of stories and poems.

Audrey Bevan, *The Years Before School*, NSW Department of Education.

Listen

I can hear the clock go tick, tick, tick,
I can hear my fingers go click, click, click,
I can hear a hammer going bang, bang, bang, bang,
I can hear the garbage lids go clang, clang, clang, clang,
Tick tick, click click, bang bang, clang clang,
Noises all around . . . listen!

Some Games With Sounds

I'm thinking of something that sounds like hat. It goes miaow. Cat!
I'm thinking of something that sounds like house. It goes eek eek. Mouse! etc.

Say Green. Green. You're a bean!
Say City. City. You're pretty.

Make up rhymes with your children's names.
Ned, Ned, stay in bed.
Alice, Alice, lives in a palace.
Laura, Laura, you're a snorer.
Nicky, Nicky, always sticky.

Animal Sounds

Make up a story about animals, using the noise of the animal instead of the name.

'Once there was a little (*snort*) with a curly tail. Now this little (*snort*) met a (*moo*) . . .'

A child who is listened to learns to listen. You child's best lessons in listening can be the example you set.

Noise

Many households suffer a high level of background noise: the washing machine, the traffic passing, the exhaust fan in the kitchen, record players, radios, the television. Children brought up in this environment are likely to 'switch off'. They hear radio and TV talk all day, and nobody seems to take much notice, so why, for example, when they go to school and a teacher talks, should they *listen?* How do you use the radio? Do you listen and appreciate it (even if you're doing the housework at the same time), or do you switch it on automatically and ignore it?

Some Noisemakers

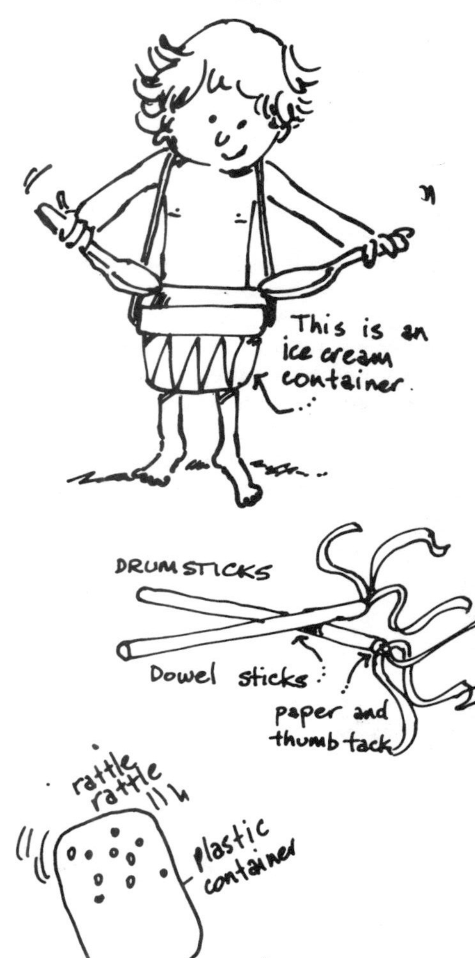

Listening to Radio

The ABC broadcasts radio programs designed for young children. You may need to help the child who has never listened before to get used to listening, responding, and 'connecting' with disembodied sounds. You can help by:

- Enjoying the session with the child, sometimes to the extent of sitting beside the radio and joining in the activities (though this makes some children self-conscious).
- Switching to it regularly. (If you're going to listen to the segments for adults involve your child in something else first.)
- Respecting the child's listening time (as you would want your listening to be respected) and avoiding interruptions and distractions.
- Keeping an ear on the program yourself so that you can learn the songs, games, etc. The child will learn more from the program if you know about it and can share things from it. The child's attention span may be short, perhaps five minutes' listening will be enough.

Listening Games

- Stop very still for a moment in the street . . . in the park . . . at the beach. What sounds can be heard?
- Make sounds yourselves. Drag a stick along a paling fence . . . along iron railings . . . listen to feet on different surfaces.
- Sit the child out of sight of what you're doing and play 'guess what is making the sound'. You could pour water into a glass . . . twirl egg beaters . . . hammer a nail . . . tear a piece of paper.
- Encourage the child to listen by giving instructions. Use words rather than showing. Give two directions at a time, then three or more.
- Record sounds and voices on a tape recorder. Talk about them. Record a sequence of sounds to make up a 'sound' story.

Hearing and Learning

In order to learn to speak effectively, a child must be able to hear properly. (Someone deaf from birth must be painstakingly *taught* to speak, and will seldom sound 'normal'). Most children naturally have very acute hearing, and from it they gather a great deal of information.

Children who cannot hear properly are likely to have all sorts of difficulties:

- They may not be safe on the streets if they cannot hear whether a car is approaching or leaving.
- They may have problems with relationships if they cannot hear vocal inflections, and distinguish anger, pleasure, or threat.
- They may have difficulty learning to read and spell if they cannot hear the differences between words: 'sound', 'round', 'mound', 'pound'.

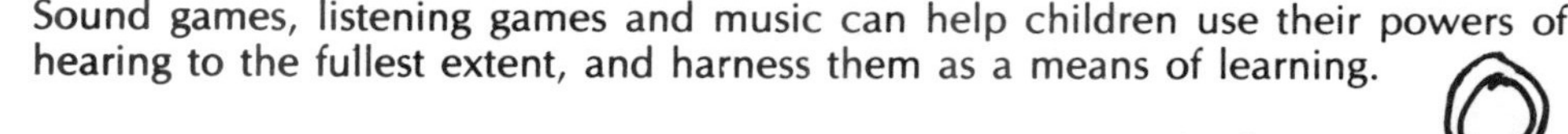

Sound games, listening games and music can help children use their powers of hearing to the fullest extent, and harness them as a means of learning.

EMOTIONS

Children are individuals, right from the moment they're born. Some are quickly upset and restless, some are placid and patient. And so it continues through life. What is easy for one is hard for another, and to expect the same behaviour from every child is unreasonable.

A child who is too controlled, and therefore prevented from engaging in behaviour normal to the particular stage of development, may be frustrated and angry. Normal 'behaviour' — even if it is the 'won't' of the two-year-old — is essential practice for life. The two-year-old *has* to practise being an independent human being. There is literature available that describes the stages of a child's development, but it is important to be sensitive to your own child, to watch and listen carefully.

Of course there will be times when the child becomes unacceptably angry or aggressive and will need to be taught what the limits are. A child can be overwhelmed by feelings. Using the words which describe the feeling can help too, then you can both consider what to do about the emotion. Everybody feels angry sometimes — it's what you *do* when you're angry that matters. If the child does something you dislike, show that what you object to is simply the action, not the person.

When you're angry, tired, upset or fussed yourself, it's very difficult to make yourself available — you tend to shut the child out. It helps to tell the child in a non-blaming way about your own feelings. That in itself relieves tension before it builds up too high.

If you're angry and you know it, stamp your feet . . .
If you're sad and you know it, have a cry . . . .

(In *Play School,* this is sometimes sung to the melody of 'Put Your Finger on your Nose')

Yelling and Squabbling

There will probably be times when a public display of emotion is undesirable, but you may just have to put up with the embarrassment. If you have allowed yourself to be drawn into a direct confrontation, defeat will severely weaken your position next time. If a child is yelling, you could suggest taking a big breath, and then another . . . yelling and breathing in at the same time are impossible.

- To avoid a squabble over division of spoils, you could try getting one child to divide them, the other to pick first. If a toy or some equipment is to be shared, try setting a kitchen timer to mark the end of one child's turn.
- Children often have a very deep sense of justice and fairness. Listen before you discipline.

Other People

If you're looking through an illustrated book or magazine with your child, you could take the opportunity to talk about the people you see and what they're doing. Are they fair or dark, short or tall, fat or thin? What are the expressions on their faces? How do they appear to be feeling?

Some people to make

DOUGH FACE

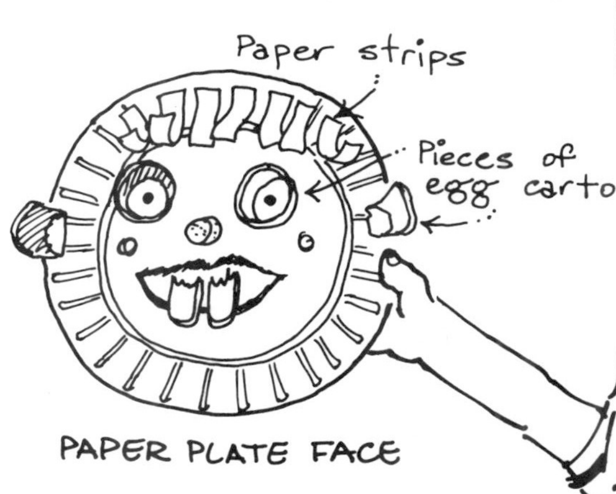

PAPER PLATE FACE

BOTTLE PERSON

Feeling Angry With Your Child

Although children bring their parents lots of joy, they may also bring frustrations and irritations. New babies cause a big change in a family's lifestyle and they certainly limit the mother's independence. They are likely to cry, vomit, or to soil at the most inconvenient times. Toddlers get into all sorts of mischief in their attempts to explore their surroundings, and two and three-year-olds usually go through a negative and disobedient stage. All of these things can be very stressful for parents, especially if they have other worries as well. Some things can be done to relieve those tensions:

- It is helpful to organise a time when you can have a complete break from the children. Don't be afraid to ask friends and relatives to do some babysitting.
- It is often very helpful just to let off steam. If you feel you can't stand the children at the moment, ring up a friend and talk about it. Crisis centres (see the front of your phone book) are happy to talk with you.
- It is important that couples share parenting. One can take over for a little while to give the other a break.
- It helps to know a little about the normal stages that all children go through, e.g., that many babies between nine and twelve months throw their food over the edge of their high chair. It is comforting to know that these are just stages and the child will pass through them.
- If the situation does not seem to get any better, talk to a doctor.

WHERE DO YOU LIVE?

Living in the City

Getting Lost

A lost child will be very frightened. No stranger will be able to provide consolation — the child will wan you. Make sure all children in your care know their full name, address and telephone number, and tel them if they get lost to go to somebody in a shop or a police officer.

Don't Forget Who You Are

*Child's name and address may be substituted

Build It Up

Now if you get the construction feeling,
You can build a tower right up to the ceiling,
And if you think that building is fun,
You can try to build a tower to the sun.

Build up one, build up two, three and four,
Are you sure you can balance on some more?
Build up five, build up six, seven and eight,
Watch it wobble like a jelly on a plate.

Some Houses to Make

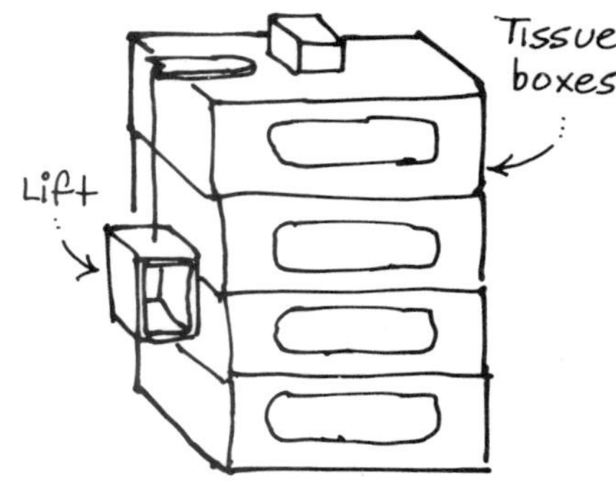

Letters and Telephones

The communications link of the mail and telephone service helps a child to understand that the lives of friends and relatives go on even though the child may only see them once or twice a year. A letter addressed just to your child can provide a thrill, especially if there are several children in the family.

As a special treat you can help your child write a 'letter' to himself or herself and post it. In a few days it should come back in the mail. What does the envelope have on it now? Where has the letter been?

Real disused telephones, toy telephones and practical 'telephones' made of tin cans or paper cups and a length of string, make good toys. By eliminating facial expression and body gesture, talking on the telephone concentrates on the verbal aspect of conversation. The child *must* use words, and when two people are playing, each must learn to listen as well as talk.

Ring Ring!

Many children like answering the telephone, though it can be disconcerting for the caller to hear monosyllabic grunts, heavy breathing, or just 'hello' — but perhaps that's what your child hears when *you* answer the phone!

HOUSES

Here's a House

G7 C G7
Here's a house with a wall, With a wall, with a wall, Here's a
G7 C
house with a floor, With a floor, with a floor, Here's a
C C7 F
house with a roof, With a roof, with a roof. (*Here's a* spoken
F# C G7
house falling down! Crash!) There's no house an - y
C C G7 C
more an - y more, There's no house an - y more.

Arranging the House

If you put treasured things out of reach, your child can move freely without cause for concern. To tell a child repeatedly, 'don't touch', is virtually to say 'don't learn'. If you allow mess in some parts of the house, you can reasonably keep other parts free of mess — and you might both manage to share the house more amicably.

A Place of One's Own

If you want your own privacy and possessions respected, perhaps you should respect your child's possessions.

- Provide a box or a washing basket for the child's own things.
- Do not insist on lending or sharing.
- Do not throw away shabby toys if they're still loved, and never put them with the garbage where they can be seen.
- As the child grows older, knock before entering his or her bedroom.

Cubby houses can be made by:

- Putting a sheet over a card table or odd bits of furniture.
- Tucking sheets around a bunk.
- Getting a huge carton from a stove or refrigerator (beg one from an appliance shop). Cut out a window and door. The child can paint it and stick on scraps of cloth for curtains with masking tape.

This is the Way

This is the way we

dust the room
sweep the floor
wash the clothes

. . . and anything else you want.

Cleaning the house

Children love to work by your side, but they know when the job isn't real. A child really can:

- Wash up. Younger ones can begin with plastic containers and unbreakable pots and pans.
- Lay the table. Valuable for learning 'one each' and left and right.
- Wash cupboard doors, refrigerators, chairs, etc. Show how to squeeze out the sponge and put lots of newspaper down for drips.
- Put away cutlery. Valuable for learning how to sort things into categories.
- Dust and vacuum. Do the two jobs together and take turns. That way the job will get done and the child will feel good.
- Wash and polish windows and mirrors. Use water in an old squeeze bottle or rag with a little methylated spirit.
- Sweep the dust into piles.
- Put away toys and clothes. But do not expect this to be done independently at first. The child likes working *with* you.

Household cleaners can be dangerous if swallowed. Keep them out of reach of toddlers.

How Many People Live at Your House?

Who really does live in your house?

Did you know that young children usually don't 'count' themselves? They find it hard to see things from a point of view other than their own.

WASHING

Helping with the washing

A child can help with the washing by:

- Sorting out dark-coloured clothes from light, for different machine loads.
- Helping to carry out the washing basket.
- Handing you the number of pegs you ask for.
- Sorting out clean clothes for each member of the family.
- Sorting the clean socks into pairs.
- Helping to fold the clothes.

While you work:

- The child can have a special bowl (or the other side of a double sink) to wash some of the child's own clothes or toys and you can string up a line to hang them on.
- Coloured plastic pegs are interesting to tip out and put back, to clip onto the sides of a tin, or a piece of cardboard, to sort into colours, to count.
- The washing basket can be a cradle, a tortoise shell, a lion's cage or a boat.
- A wooden block makes a substitute iron.

Children and irons should be kept apart.

'Mind you don't get dirty' is a hangover from the days when washing and ironing were major productions. If you're out, it's easier to take along a bib or a clean shirt and do a little extra washing than to nag and frustrate your child, and upset yourself.

Wet Washing

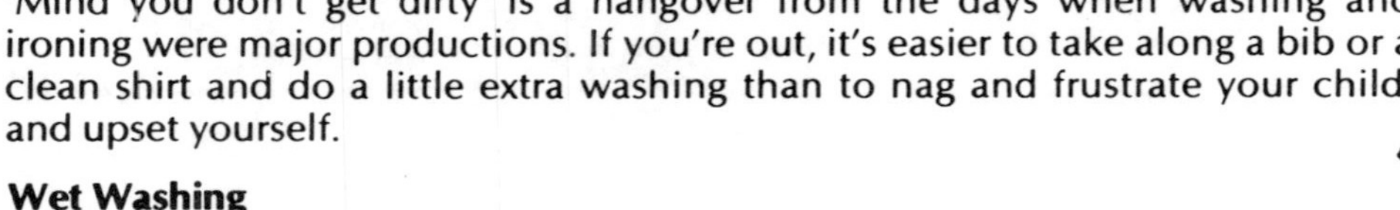

Dolly Peg People

If you can still find the old-fashioned wooden dolly pegs, they make good people. Draw on the faces, and dress them in scraps of material held with a rubber band. If you want to stand them up, wedge their 'feet' into dough or plasticene. Arms can be made by winding a pipe cleaner round the neck, and hair by sticking on a few scraps of wool.

Bubbles

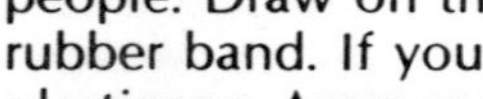

Blowing Bubbles

Use a plastic drinking straw, and a container filled with soap flakes and water. Show the child how to blow, not suck (three-year-olds can learn to manage it). Are there colours in the bubbles? What shape are the bubbles?

To make bubbles that float in the air, add a little cooking oil to the mixture. The child can experiment with things to blow through — an old-fashioned key, a looped pipe cleaner, a slotted spoon, fingers in the shape of an '0'. Will a fork work?

Bath time

A bath soothes an excited child and comforts a tired one. (You may find a bath or shower improves *your* mood too!)

Bath Time

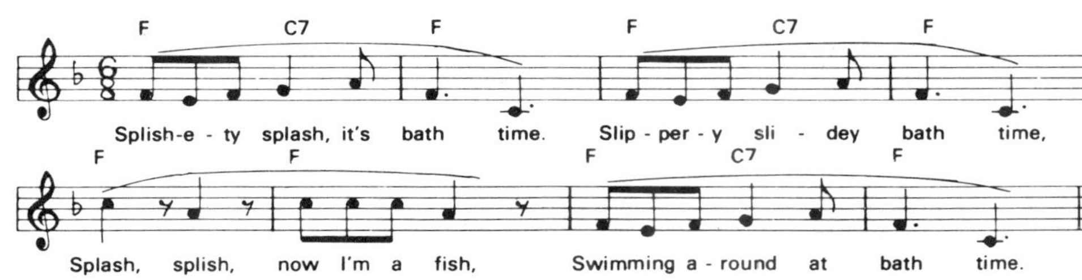

Rub a dub dub, it's towel time,
Pit a pat pit, it's towel time,
Rub a dub dry,
And powder till I
Am warm and sweet at towel time.

In the bathroom, it is pleasant to have somewhere comfortable to sit so that you can talk to the occupant of the bath, and to have interesting equipment for experiments with water. This equipment can include:

- A soap dish or bath toys to float.
- A squeezy bottle to fill and squirt.
- A sponge to absorb water and squeeze it out.
- Clear tubing to bubble through and syphon.
- A sieve, a funnel and a plastic jug for pouring.
- A plastic string bag to put them all away in.

If your child is unaccustomed to a shower and you find yourself in a place where there's no bath, you could go into the shower too. It will give the child confidence — and it feels pleasant.
Show that you love and value *all* of the child's body and use the correct terms so that the child is familiar and at ease with the names of parts of the body.

Never leave a child under five alone in the bath – not even for a moment to answer the phone.

Hair Washing

Some children hate having their hair washed. You could try:

- Finding a shampoo which doesn't sting the eyes.
- Having a flexible hand shower.
- Protecting the child's eyes with swimming goggles.
- Protecting the child's ears with ear plugs.
- Laying the child along the kitchen bench with head hanging backwards over the sink.
- Inviting a child who enjoys having hair washed to share hair washing time. You could wash your own hair at the same time.

Cleaning Teeth

A child should have a toothbrush with soft bristles and a small head. The bristles should be aimed at the gumline and jiggled or moved in tiny circles. An electric toothbrush is fun and very efficient. Fluoride toothpaste helps prevent tooth decay. A child under ten may find it hard to clean teeth thoroughly without help. Perhaps once a day you could help with tooth-cleaning.

Department of Preventive Dentistry, University of Sydney.

IN THE KITCHEN

You probably spend quite a lot of time in the kitchen, and your child will want to be where you are. Here are some jobs your child can help you with:

- Chopping vegetables, such as zucchini or celery. Make sure to have a knife that does the job but won't cut little fingers.
- Breaking eggs (unless you want to separate the whites from the yolks!).
- Beating eggs, pancake mixture, etc.
- Sieving flour.
- Pouring in milk, etc., as you mix.

Try to set up the kitchen so that there is space for the child to work without being in the way. Make available a special drawer or shelf where the child can have safe tools.

A child's kitchen tools could include:

- Pots and pans of different sizes to stack, nest or fit lids to.
- A plastic jug and funnel for pouring.
- Assorted plastic containers.
- A sieve or colander.
- A washing-up bowl.
- Lots of implements to create sounds with – wooden and metal spoons, plastic boxes, metal lids.

The Kitchen Symphony

Take two lids and make them clash,
Wooden spoon on saucepan bash,
Knives and forks ring out with dings,
The Kitchen Symphony begins!

Bang bang clash clash bang bang ding-a-ding bang clash clash bang bang tock tock ting ting bang bang bubble bubble rubarub whirr whirr ting tock whirr whirr rubarub ding whirr splash splash bang CLASH!

Make up a story about:

What other characters lurk in your cupboards?

Keep out of reach:
Sharp knives. Electric cords. Hot saucepans. Household cleaners and detergents. Plastic bags large enough to go over a child's head.

I'm a Little Teapot

I'm a tube of toothpaste on the shelf
I get so lonely, here by myself
When it comes to night-time, then I shout,
'Just lift my lid off, squeeze me out.'

I'm a little robot, short and square,
I have no toenails, I have no hair,
If you want the answer to a sum,
Just press my button, out it comes.

Playing Tea Parties

- Cups and saucers can be made from parts of egg cartons.
- Mats can be sheets of paper folded in four and then torn to make interesting patterns.
- Food can be dough, or pictures cut from old magazines. Perhaps you have bits and pieces around the house you don't mind the child using – paper flowers, a small metal teapot or coasters.
- A play stove can be made with a cardboard box. Draw the hot plates and switches with a felt pen or stick on lids, paper plates, bottle tops, etc. Pots and pans can be made with foil pie plates. Stick on wooden iceblock sticks for handles.
- You can make a stemmed glass for a tiny doll out of a sweet paper. Silver paper or coloured cellophane ones are the best. Wrap it round your finger for the cup, twist for the stem, and splay out the base.

Polly Put the Kettle On

COOKING

Children enjoy cooking; the result is a useful product, and the process provides rich learning experiences – how much, how hot, how wet; how things change, smell, taste; how to stir, beat, spread, shape or cut. Of course cooking with children requires patience, continuous supervision, a positive approach to accidents and disasters and some basic rules, but it can be one of the most challenging and satisfying activities around the home for children of both sexes.

Accidents will happen, and children can learn from them – how they happened, what the results were, and how to prevent future ones. Until a child actually sees what happens, for example, when an egg is dropped on the kitchen floor, it is hard to understand why eggs must be carried carefully.

For burns and scalds, apply plenty of cold water. Do not use any ointment or other substance. If severe, wrap the child in a clean sheet and go straight to hospital.

Kitchen Procedures

- Make sure you both have plenty of space – floor space and bench space. Cramping can lead to frayed tempers.
- Wash hands.
- Put on aprons – or be prepared for floury tummies.
- Teach respect for heat.
- Try to give the child challenging but possible jobs so that you don't have to take over to achieve an edible product. (Children need to *succeed* in order to develop positive self-regard).
- Involve the child in cleaning up afterwards.

Recipes

Pikelets

2 teaspoons butter
1 cup self-raising flour
pinch salt
2 teaspoons sugar
1 egg
½ cup milk

Melt the butter. Put it into a bowl with the flour, the salt, the sugar, the egg, about half a cup of milk and the melted butter. Stir it all up until there are no lumps. You may need to add more milk. Grease the griddle or frypan. Drop the mixture on in spoonfuls. When the pikelet is bubbly, turn it over and cook the other side. (Watch out for the child's wrists on the hot edge of the frypan.)

Bread

1 teaspoon sugar
1 tablespoon loosely crumbled compressed yeast
⅓ cup lukewarm water
2½ cups plain wholemeal flour
1 teaspoon salt
1 teaspoon honey
1 cup milk
sesame or poppy seeds

Combine sugar, yeast, and lukewarm water and stand in a warm place for 5-10 minutes, or until frothy. Mix flour, salt and honey in a bowl. Add yeast mixture, and milk (heated to almost blood temperature) to flour and stir thoroughly with a wooden spoon until mixed. Knead on a lightly floured table for 10 minutes, or until dough becomes firm and pliable. Place in a bowl, stand in a warm place for 40 minutes or until doubled in bulk. Knead dough lightly, mould into desired shape and stand in a warm place for 10-15 minutes. Sprinkle with sesame or poppy seeds. Bake in a hot oven (220°C) for 30 minutes. (Children can help flour the table; then hands will be ready for the kneading. Banging and squeezing the dough to knead it are fun.)

Gingerbread Men

1 cup flour
½ teaspoon soda
2 teaspoons ground ginger
½ cup sugar
125 g butter
1 egg

Sift flour, soda and ginger together. Beat the butter and sugar. Add the beaten egg, then fold in the sifted dry ingredients. Shape into gingerbread men. Decorate and cook 20 minutes at 200°C.

Butter

carton of cream
salt if required

Beat the cream in a large bowl until flecks of butter appear. Pour off the milk (buttermilk) and mash the butter together into a ball. Add salt if required.

Plain Biscuits

½ cup sugar
½ cup butter
1 egg, beaten
few drops vanilla essence
2 cups plain flour
1 teaspoon baking powder
cherries, almonds, sultanas or currants for decoration

Beat sugar and butter. Add the beaten egg slowly, beating all the time. Add the vanilla. Add sifted flour and baking powder. Place on floured board and roll out. Cut into shapes and decorate. Put on greased biscuit slide and cook at 190°C for 10-15 minutes. Allow to cool on the slide.

The sweet food eaten between meals does the most damage to teeth. Such food can be confined to mealtimes, and the teeth brushed afterwards.

I'm So Hungry

A baby squeezing banana through his fingers is conducting a scientific experiment.

A lunchbox might have in it:

- A protein rich food.
- A fruit or vegetable.
- A drink.
- A message.

Eating

Sometimes all sorts of feelings are attached to eating — loving ones, angry ones, hostile ones. Mealtimes can develop into a power struggle between parent and child. If mealtimes become upsetting, the child won't feel like eating.

- Offer your child good healthy food and present it in an interesting and varied way.
- Don't be anxious about whether food is eaten or not.
- Children should be allowed to feed themselves as soon as possible.
- Try to give a choice of suitable alternatives.
- Don't worry too much about food fads. Most don't last.
- Try to establish an agreed pattern of family behaviour. Mealtimes are an excellent opportunity for the child to learn from the rest of the family. If everyone is watching television or reading the paper, that opportunity is lost.

Interesting food

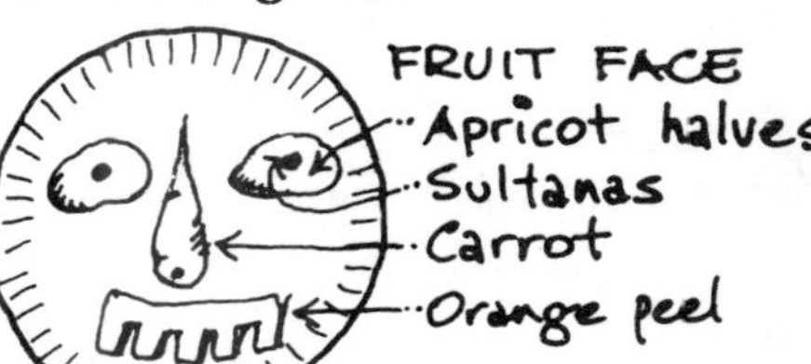

A 'Food' story

There was once a boy whose mother told him to look for a little red house with no windows, no doors, a chimney on top, and a beautiful star inside. He searched and searched, and at last he found:

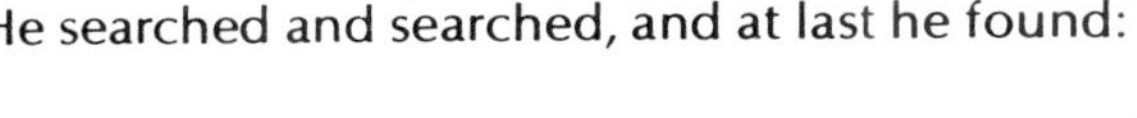

CLOTHES

Put On Your . . .

A song to be sung while the child dresses. Adapt to shirt, pants, dress, etc., and use the appropriate colour instead of 'new'.

Getting Dressed

A child likes to do things without help and most people want their children to be competent and independent. If a child is learning to dress without help:

- Provide time and opportunity to practise.
- There needs to be a fair chance of succeeding in the job being attempted.
- Remember to praise success.

To avoid hassles over what to wear, put out a limited selection of clothes, *any* of which is suitable, and allow the child to choose.

Ready for School

A child needs to be able to dress and undress without help before starting school. You can help by providing:

- Shoes and socks that are easy to manage.
- Trousers with elastic waistbands.
- Clothes with zips or buttons at the front or side.
- Clothes labelled in a way that both child and teacher will recognise.

Avoiding Knotty Hair Horrors

- Use a good shampoo and conditioner.
- Try using your fingers to untangle knots.
- When combing, tease out the ends first, then work up to the scalp.

Have you shown your child how a comb attracts a small light object such as a scrap of paper after picking up electricity from hair?

Making Clothes

If you sew or knit, don't do it only at night when the child can't see you. Children love to know you value them enough to make things for them. And they can sew with you.

What Will I Be Today?

C C# Dm7 G7
What do you think I should be to - day? I'm
Dm7 G7 C C7 F F#
dres - sing up, it's time to play. What will I be —— ?
C A7 D7 G7 C
What do you say —— ? What will I be to - day?

For playing: wear clothes that won't constrict and tangle.
In the bush: wear shoes.
In the hot sun: wear a hat.

A button box will provide endless opportunities for sorting and threading, but keep buttons away from babies who still put things in their mouths.

A Dressing-up Box

A child often likes dressing up for its own sake, not necessarily to 'be' anything at all. You can put aside a drawer, perhaps, or an old suitcase, a washing basket, or a cardboard box for dressing-up clothes. You could put in old trousers (cut off the bottoms), dresses, handbags, hats of all sorts, shoes or scarves.

I Am the King

A king or queen might wear an old curtain or bedspread for a cloak, a crown cut from a paper bag, or a more elaborate one made out of strips of cardboard. Jewellery can be silver or gold milk bottle tops, or pieces of aluminium foil.
An Arab might wear a teatowel with a hairband on top.
A firefighter's hat could be a sou'wester.
A diver might wear a skivvy and tights, egg carton goggles, and tissue boxes for his flippers and air tank.
A singer might wear a necklace of macaroni threaded on string. Long hair can be made by cutting strips in a sheet of newspaper, or by using the top part of a pair of panty hose. Cut off the legs and fringe the rest up to the waistband.

Bananas in Pyjamas

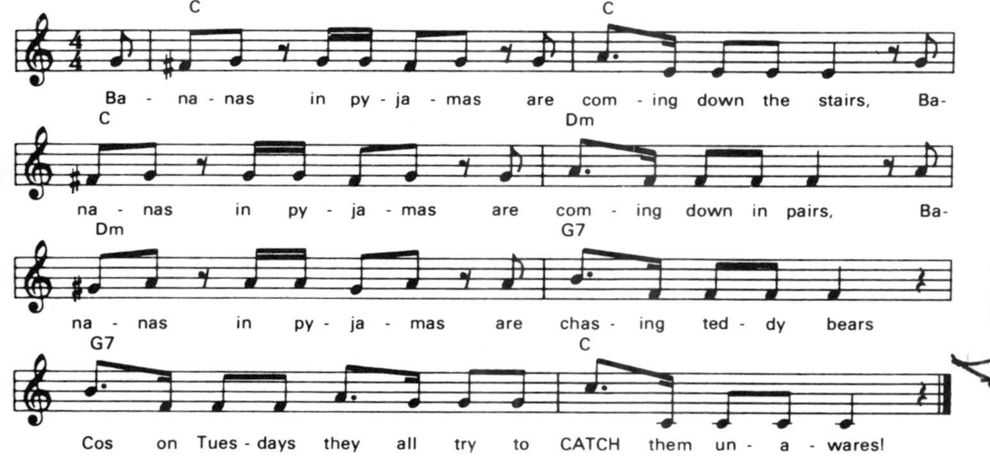

PAINTING

Painting is:
- Fun.
- A way of communicating.
- A learning experience.

Painting encourages:
- Creativity.
- Muscular co-ordination.
- Language development.
- Sharing and co-operation.
- Visual discrimination, perception of spatial relations and use of concepts such as small, big, bigger.

Equipment

Paint
Paint should be thick and plentiful and the colours rich. Plastic paint in tubes, powdered poster colour or tempera are suitable. Use three or four colours at a time (each with its own brush). Paint should be washable.

Finger paint
Mix one heaped tablespoon of cornflour with a little water till you get a smooth milky paste. Pour on some boiling water, stirring *very* quickly, until it turns thick, clear and smooth. If it doesn't thicken, you may need to cook it for a little while. Add a little paint, dye or food colouring – the brighter the better. Allow to cool before the child uses it. A little detergent mixed into the paint makes cleaning off easier.

Paper
Paper does *not* have to be expensive drawing paper. You could use:
- Butcher's paper.
- Wallpaper lining.
- The backs of wallpaper samples.
- Brown wrapping paper.
- The sides of cardboard cartons.
- Newspaper (the small advertisements).
- Computer printouts and other discarded business paper.

Tools
These include thick brushes, thick pencils, thick crayons and thick washable felt pens. (It is important that these be thick, as they can be grasped more easily by small fingers whose muscular co-ordination is not yet fully developed.) Old shirts turned back to front make good painting aprons.

Some Ways to Make Pictures

Blow painting
Put a drop of food colouring on a sheet of paper (not too large, as this can be tiring) then blow through a drinking straw to move the colour in different directions across the page.

String patterns
Dip a piece of string (about 20 cm long) into some thick paint until it is completely covered. Fold a sheet of paper in half, open it out again and drop the paint-covered string onto one side of the paper in a pattern, leaving one end of the string over the edge. Fold the paper over again and hold it down with one hand. Pull out the string. Now open the paper. For more interesting patterns, use more than one piece of string, and two colours.

Vegetable printing
Try printing with an onion or lemon cut in half, a slice of cauliflower or a potato cut out to make a shape.

Hand, foot and finger printing
Use thick paint in an old dish or plate. Dip fingertips, thumbtips, hands or feet into the paint, and press lightly onto a sheet of paper.

Body painting
Use the finger paint recipe, or ordinary water soluble paint. Body and face painting can carry over into role play and drama.

Finger painting
Daub some paint directly onto the paper and allow the child to swish and swirl the paint around. Or you could put the paint on a wet, non-porous surface such as a vinyl-topped table. After the child has made the painting, lay a sheet of paper over the paint and lift it off for a permanent record of the work.

Spot Song

You could put a stripe, a swirl, a blob or anything you like.

Colour Mixing Experiments

1. You will need:
- Food colouring (the primaries – red, yellow, blue).
- An eye-dropper.
- Some jar lids.

The child can experiment by mixing a few drops of each colour on the lids.

2. You will need:
- Food colouring mixed with water (baby food jars are ideal containers).
- Cotton balls.
- Absorbent paper.

The child can dip the cotton balls in the colours and make pictures or patterns on the paper.

3. You will need:
- Two balls of playdough, of different colours.

The child can model using the colours separately or in combination.

When a child is painting:
- Take an interest in it.
- Establish an area where the child can work, free from adult interference and censure.
- Have a place where the child's work can be displayed, e.g., in the kitchen on the cupboards or the refrigerator, on the end of a cupboard or wardrobe in the child's room.
- Encourage the child to clean up afterwards.
- Encourage the child to talk about the painting *before* you comment.

It is sometimes hard to ask sensible questions about a child's picture. Sometimes a child likes to put colour on paper because it looks and feels good at the time, so beware of 'overkill' with questions. However, here are some open-ended ones you might try:
- Tell me about your picture.
- Who is in the picture?
- What is happening?
- (If the child is in the picture) Who is with you? What is (the other person) doing? What are you doing?
- Where do you see patterns like that?

After you have some idea of what the child has painted, you might stimulate language use with further questions, e.g. :

What would happen next?
What happened when you mixed red with blue?
How did the dough feel when you were mixing it?

Playdough can be used for:
Rolling
Cutting
Making shapes
Pounding
Kneading
Mixing
Sharing, baking, modelling

Playdough recipes

Playdough is clean to use and cheap and easy to make.

Uncooked playdough

1 cup plain flour
¼ cup salt
1 tablespoon cooking oil
a few drops of food colouring
½ cup water

Mix the flour and salt together. Add the oil. Add the food colouring to the water, then add the coloured liquid, a little at a time, to the flour mixture. Knead until the mixture is smooth and has the consistency of scone dough. Multiply the quantity by the number of children using the dough. Children can mix this themselves.

Cooked playdough

4 cups flour
1 cup salt
1 small packet cream of tartar
1 tablespoon oil
4 cups water
food colouring if required

Mix flour, salt and cream of tartar. Add oil and water, stirring. Cook slowly until mixture thickens, stirring continuously. Store in an airtight container. This playdough will keep for about three months. It has a smoother consistency than the uncooked dough.

TELEVISION

The way in which a young child perceives television is different from the way in which an adult perceives it.

Viewing television with a child

- Young children see a series of separate and fragmentary incidents, rather than the story of a television film.
- The content of these incidents suggests that children will see either all good or all bad characters.
- It is likely that the three- and four-year-old child will not invariably recognise the identities of the principal characters throughout the film. The perception of the film characters is dominated by the setting in which they are filmed.
- Moreover, young children tend to believe implicitly what they see on television to be real.
- Young children while viewing may read incidents into the plot from their own imaginations, or add incidents and events that they think should have occurred.
- It seems likely that young children will use television programs as the basis for social play, although such play is likely to be of a highly stereotyped nature.
- Children may acquire their future how-to-behave models from watching television. Young children are excellent mimics of what they see on the television screen.

From Grant Noble, *Children in Front of the Small Screen*, Constable, 1975

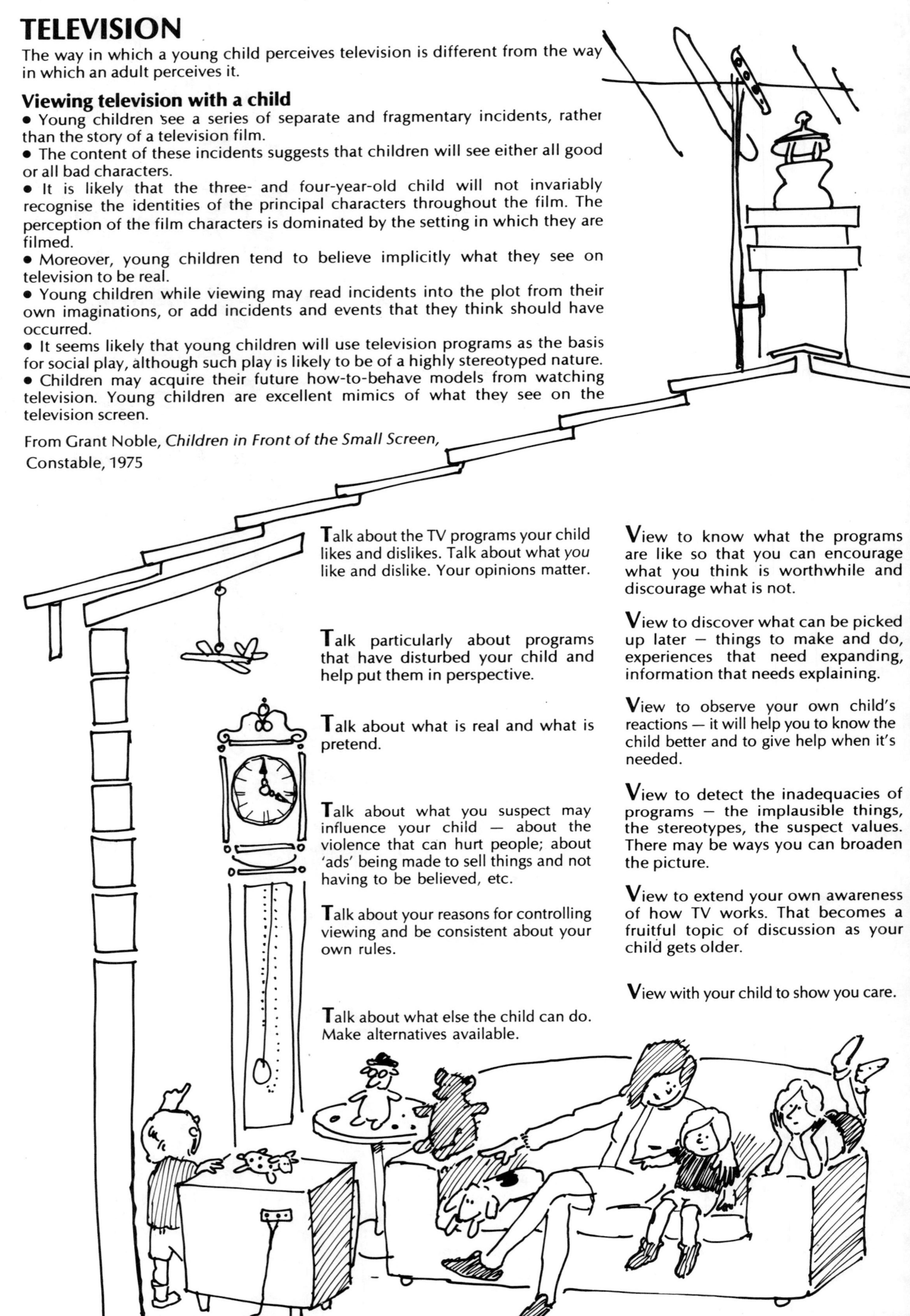

Talk about the TV programs your child likes and dislikes. Talk about what *you* like and dislike. Your opinions matter.

Talk particularly about programs that have disturbed your child and help put them in perspective.

Talk about what is real and what is pretend.

Talk about what you suspect may influence your child — about the violence that can hurt people; about 'ads' being made to sell things and not having to be believed, etc.

Talk about your reasons for controlling viewing and be consistent about your own rules.

Talk about what else the child can do. Make alternatives available.

View to know what the programs are like so that you can encourage what you think is worthwhile and discourage what is not.

View to discover what can be picked up later — things to make and do, experiences that need expanding, information that needs explaining.

View to observe your own child's reactions — it will help you to know the child better and to give help when it's needed.

View to detect the inadequacies of programs — the implausible things, the stereotypes, the suspect values. There may be ways you can broaden the picture.

View to extend your own awareness of how TV works. That becomes a fruitful topic of discussion as your child gets older.

View with your child to show you care.

Some ways to help a child understand how television works

- Make a toy TV set out of a cardboard box for your child to 'put on TV shows', perhaps using toys or puppets, or cutting pictures out of magazines. This activity will help a child understand that TV shows are 'performances'.
- Mention the 'ads' as 'ads' so that the child can begin to differentiate between them and the program content.
- Show a picture with a magnifying glass to help explain how a 'close-up' works.
- Make a 'flip-book' to help show how cartoons work (and if you have any film equipment, let the child draw on a length of exposed film with a felt pen, and project it).
- Show the picture in the front of this book and talk about it. If possible, give the child 'direct' experience with the media.
- Help the child understand the concept of recording. If you take photographs or home movies, the child will understand that images can be captured. If you have a tape recorder, let the child do some recording.
- Visit a television studio, or somewhere where video equipment is being displayed so that you can see yourselves on a screen, and so learn that people on screen are not actually in the television set.

Relate these 'how-they-do-it' ideas to familiar programs.

This is how a flip book works

- Start with the next page and flip back to page 80 You will see our little inchworm inching its way off the page.

You can do this with a series of thin cards held with a bulldog clip

Use a "stick figure" if you like or make a ball bounce ....

The Play School Song

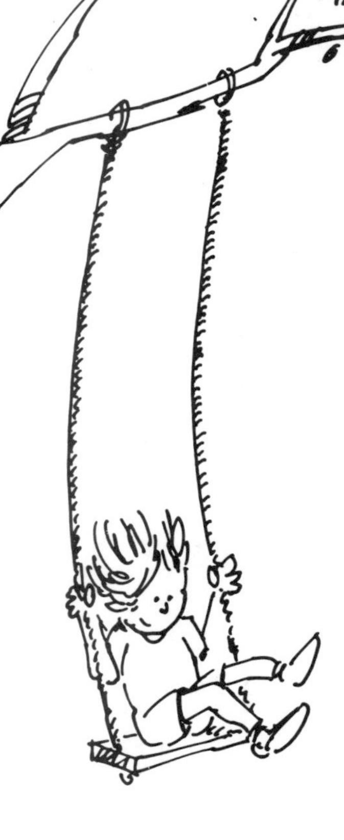

FEELING SICK

Coping with a sick child

This takes:
- Love — the child may just want the warmth and security of a familiar person nearby, or a special toy.
- Understanding — there may be worries about the changes sickness brings about and the child will possibly behave as a much younger child would.
- Patience — the child may be very demanding, and very irritable!

I Feel Sick!

2 I have a nasty headache
And my teeth are very sore,
My tongue looks most peculiar
And my eyes are red and raw,
My nose is feeling funny
And my ears twitch more and more,
I feel sick! I feel sick!

Playing with a sick child in bed

- We can feel so sorry for sick children that we want to 'make it up' to them by giving them anything they want (or we think they want). The sick child will probably prefer just a special toy, a few playthings changed around and then used again the next day, and *lots* of time and attention.
- You may find it difficult to cope with the patient and get your work done. How essential is the work? Try moving your child to a bed in the living room, or do jobs like ironing or sewing where you can be seen. Put the TV nearby and watch too.
- If possible, try some 'messy' play, e.g., painting, dough, etc. An old shower curtain on the bed and an old shirt on the patient will keep both reasonably clean. A breakfast tray with legs makes a good work table.

Miss Polly

He looked at the dolly and he shook his head
He said, 'Miss Polly, put her straight to bed'.
He wrote on the paper for a pill, pill, pill,
'I'll be back in the morning with my bill, bill, bill.'

Children sometimes use play to come to terms with their own experiences. A sick child might like:

- An amenable doll or teddy.
- A First Aid box (an old shoe box), containing:
  iceblock sticks and rubber bands to make splints for broken limbs
  plastic straws cut in half for thermometers
  sticking plasters
  large handkerchiefs or old nappies for slings or nurses' hats
  a bandage, or a strip of old sheeting
  a large safety pin
  an empty pill bottle
  a toy stethoscope
  some cotton wool

An ambulance can be made out of a box. Make sure it has a light and a siren.

When giving medicine, follow the instructions and give *only* the recommended dose. Keep medicines out of reach.

Put ear in here

Going to Hospital

Before going to hospital:

- Tell the child about the illness, and talk about what will happen in hospital. You'll lose trust if you promise that medicine tastes nice, or the doctor won't hurt, and it proves untrue.
- Take the family to visit the ward where the child is to be admitted. That will help you to answer everyone's questions (and the sick child may ask them again and again, because of feeling upset).
- Let the child help to pack a bag with special 'things'. Don't forget a favourite toy, which can be a valuable link between home and hospital.

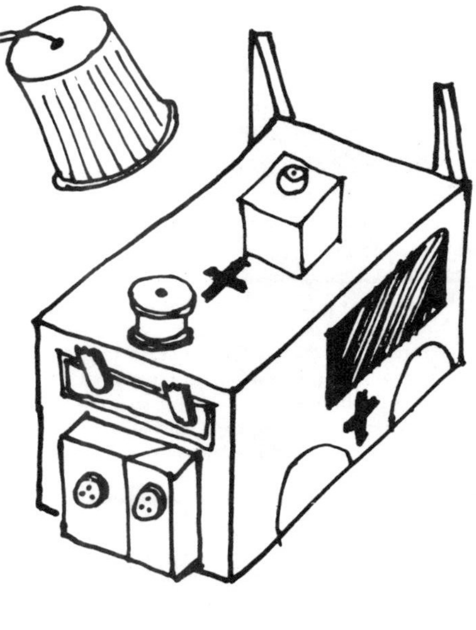

In Hospital

- The very young child's greatest worry is the possibility of being separated from loved family members. Hospital is probably unfamiliar and frightening, so spend as much time as you can with the child. Many hospitals have live-in facilities for parents and unrestricted visiting hours.
- If you have to leave and your child becomes upset, remember this is a normal protest and it mustn't deter you from visiting. Alert a staff member to offer consolation and leave promptly, telling the child when you will return. (Keep your promise!)
- Don't neglect other children in the family in your concern for the sick child. They may well worry. Take them to visit and explain to them why their brother or sister is in hospital.

THE BACK YARD

Whether you have a big garden, a tiny yard, or just a balcony, you can give your child the opportunity to play with dirt or with sand and water and to watch things grow. For a few years you may have to choose between a perfect garden and a learning-place for your child.

Sand

Sand and water might have been created for children to play with. Dry sand can be sifted, poured, trickled through the fingers, scrunched between the toes. Add water, watch the texture change, shape it, mould it, pile it, dig in it, make handprints and footprints. Draw in it. Make roads, bridges, castles or lakes.

A carton or an old baby bath full of sand is better than nothing, but a good sandpit is well worth building, if you have the space. It will provide endless pleasure and learning experiences for children of all ages. (Cats like sandpits too — plastic sheeting pulled over at night will keep them off).

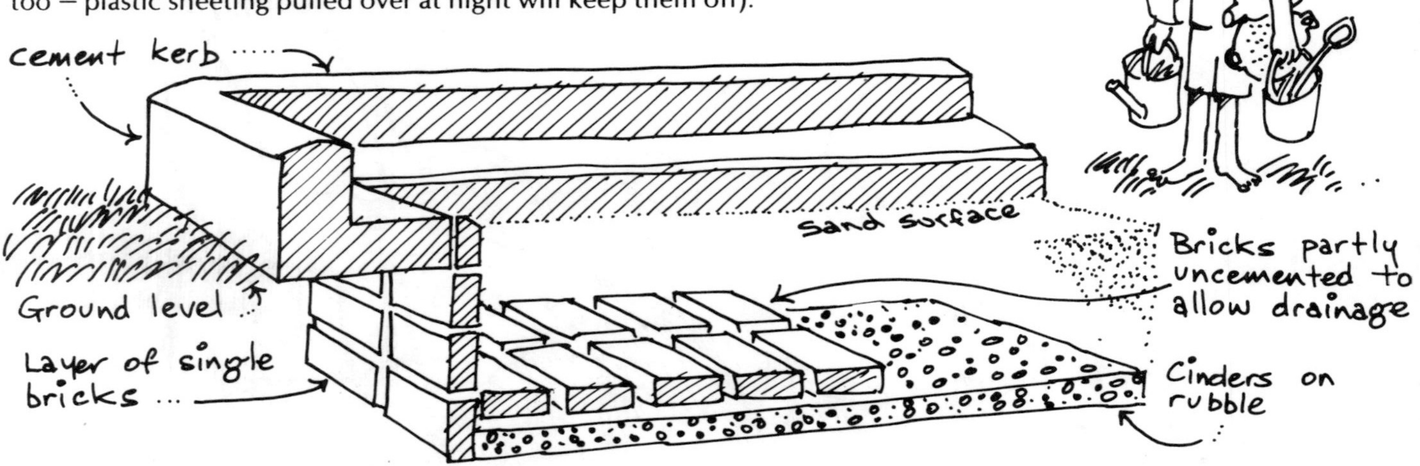

Sandpit tools could include:
- Big metal or wooden spoons to dig with. Plastic icecream containers.
- An old sieve or colander.
- You can make a good scoop out of a plastic bottle. Sandpaper or file the sharp edges, or bind them with tape.
- Have a tap or hose within reach, or just a bucket of water.

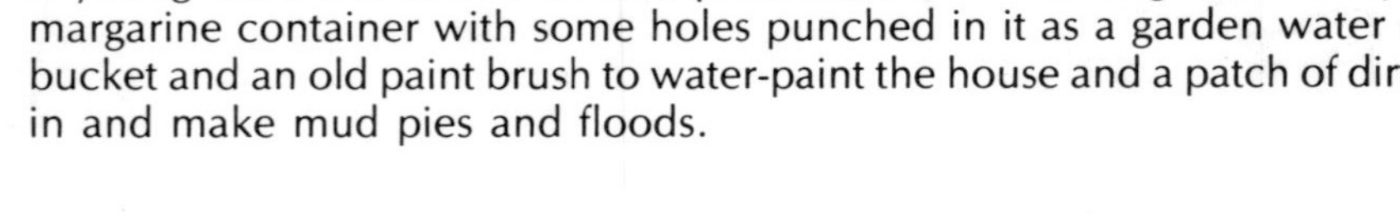

Water

A young child will derive endless pleasure from a trickling hose or tap. Provide a margarine container with some holes punched in it as a garden water sprinkler, a bucket and an old paint brush to water-paint the house and a patch of dirt to squelch in and make mud pies and floods.

Back Yard Equipment

Try to provide basic equipment for your child and any friends to build and jump and scramble and climb, to make cubby houses, to make boats and cars, fire engines and aeroplanes. Most things can be obtained at no cost at all. Watch out for splinters and protruding nails, and guard against spiders.

You could have:
- Tyres (an old tractor tyre cut in half is good for water play).
- Cartons, fruit boxes, large packing cases.
- One or two planks.
- Wooden cable reels.
- A climbing net.
- An old baby bath or paddle pool.

It is irresponsible not to have a back yard swimming pool fenced. Always have something that will float close by, to throw into the pool in an emergency. Even a child who can swim still needs supervision. Empty a wading pool after use, a child can drown in a small amount of water.

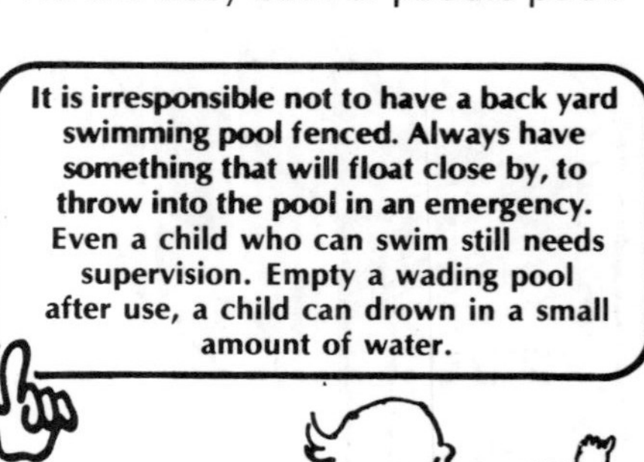

Gardening

A child learns by being with you, watching you, helping. While you do *your* work try to find satisfying and interesting jobs for the child to do alongside, perhaps:

- Snip off dead flower heads.
- Rake up after the mower (but keep children away while you are mowing in case the blades throw up stones).
- Water the garden.
- Dig in the dirt (a hand trowel is more satisfying than a toy implement).
- Have a special garden. An old double sink or bathtub makes an ideal child's garden. Stand it on bricks to raise it off the ground. Cover the bottom with a layer of stones to let the water drain through, and fill with soil. You could plant seeds to form a shape, or the initial letter of the child's name.

It's probably easier to watch things grow in a pot or jar than out in the garden.

- Onions will shoot in a glass jar. Find an onion which just wedges into the neck of a jar. Fill the jar with water up to the bottom of the onion, and leave it in a dark place (to simulate the darkness under the earth) until it begins to shoot. Then transfer it to a light sunny place.
- Sweet potatoes may be grown in the same way.
- Dried beans will shoot in damp blotting paper. Soak them overnight first.
- Pips — orange, lemon, grapefruit, avocado — can be planted in plastic yoghurt pots. Make a small hole in the bottom and put in a few little stones for drainage. Fill with soil or potting mix. (You won't get a fruit-bearing tree, but if you plant a few pips at a time, one *might* come up. If you want to be sure, though, plant a packet of seeds.)

Don't leave garden tools lying around. Pesticides should be securely out of reach.

Watch out ....

Pressing Flowers

Lay them out on blotting paper and cover with another piece of blotting paper. Press with a heavy book (such as the telephone book) for three days. You can stick them (using a very little glue) on a piece of coloured card, and cover over with clear plastic for a present.

One Potato

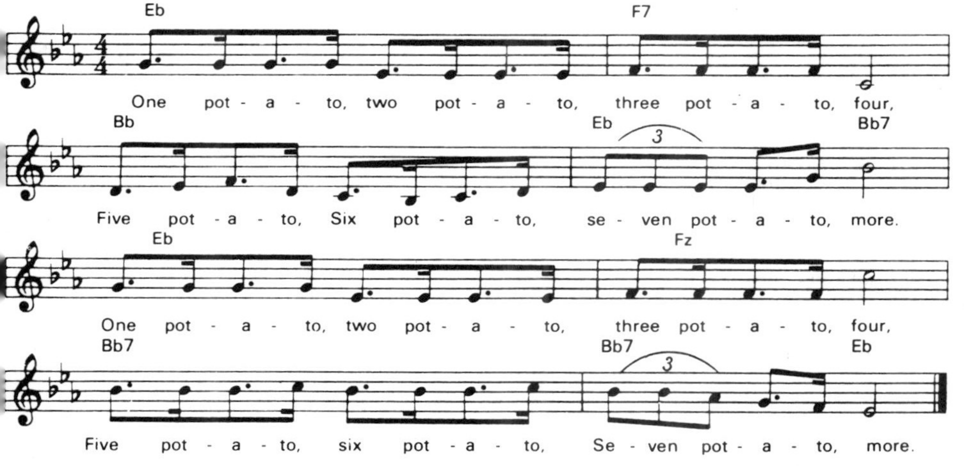

Birds

Two Little Dickie Birds

Two little dickie birds
Sitting on a wall,
One called Peter,
One called Paul.
Fly away, Peter,
Fly away, Paul,
Come back, Peter,
Come back, Paul.

Peter Paul

No Peter No Paul

Have you and your child ever:

- Smelt the honey in honeysuckle or clover?
- Made a daisy chain?
- Looked for a four-leaved clover?
- Made a lei from frangipani flowers?
- Told the time by a dandelion puff?
- Made a snapdragon snap?
- Turned a fuchsia flower into a ballerina?
- Shot with a plantain gun?
- Made a little doll from a poppy flower?
- Used a buttercup to tell whether each of you likes butter?
- Scrunched and shuffled through autumn leaves?
- Looked closely at a spider's web?

Even if you have a cat you can still have the pleasure of birds in the garden or on a balcony. Put out food regularly (out of a cat's reach), preferably near a window from which you can watch the birds as they feed.

BACK YARD CREATURES

How Does a Caterpillar Go?

How could other animals go?

Give a butterfly kiss by blinking your eyelashes against the child's cheek.

Caterpillars and Butterflies

Summer is the time when a caterpillar turns into a chrysalis. If you find a chrysalis, put it in an airy box and wait for it to hatch out into a butterfly — or a moth.

To make paper butterflies:

- Drip gooey paint onto paper.
- Fold the paper in half and press it.
- Cut out a butterfly shape.
- Open up the paper butterfly.

Make lots and hang them on cotton for a butterfly mobile.

Spiders

Eency Weency Spider

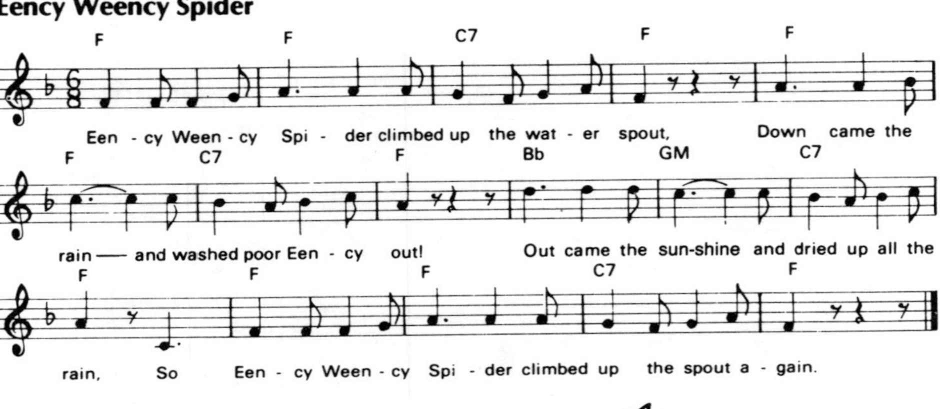

Little Miss Muffet

Teach children not to handle spiders.

These spiders are poisonous:

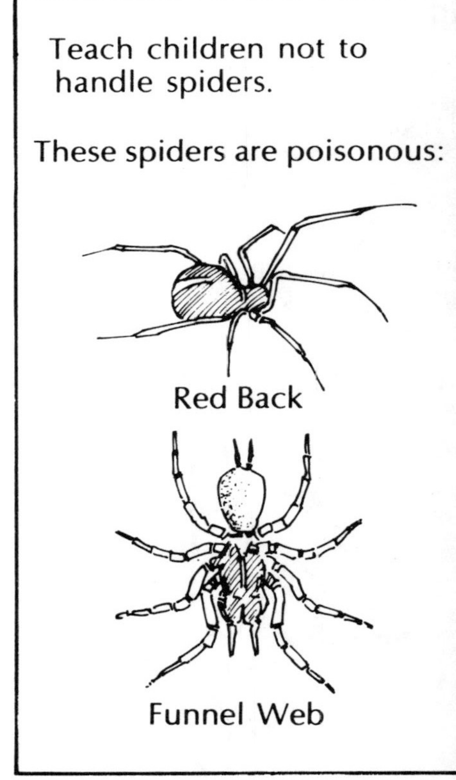

Red Back

Funnel Web

There is a fine line between alerting children to potential dangers and making them too terrified to enjoy and explore their surroundings. Your own calm, sensible attitude is crucial. If the situation is genuinely frightening to both of you, you can share your feelings and gain reassurance together.

Bees

What do you suppose?
A bee sat on my nose.
Then what do you think?
He gave me a wink,
And said, 'I beg your pardon,
I thought you were the garden!'

Here is the Beehive

Here is the beehive, where are the bees?
Hid - ing a - way where no - bod - y sees.
Watch them come creep - ing out of their hive,
1 and 2 and 3, 4, 5!

Take time to watch:

- Ants carrying spilt sugar back to their nest.
- Dug-up worms writhing to get back under the dark earth.
- A caterpillar moving along a leaf. Do all caterpillars move in the same way?
- A lizard lying in the sun. What is it waiting for?
- A snail stretching and contracting as it moves. Touch one of its feelers very gently.

Look at its underside by putting it on a transparent surface.

A big-mouthed frog can be made out of a paper plate folded in half. Staple on two bug eyes from an egg carton.

Frogs

Mister Frog

Mis - ter Frog jumped out of his pond one day, And found him - self in the rain. Said he, I'll get wet and I might catch cold — A - choo! So he jumped in the pond a - gain.

PETS

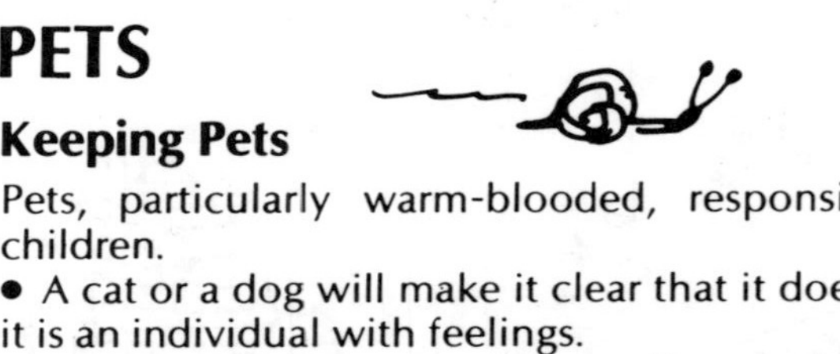

Keeping Pets

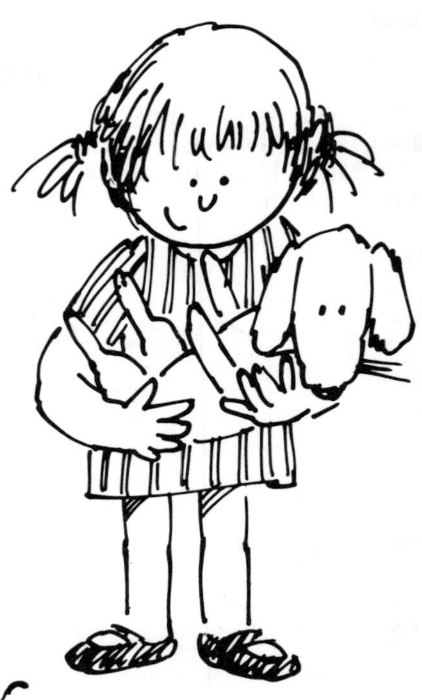

Pets, particularly warm-blooded, responsive ones, have much to teach children.

- A cat or a dog will make it clear that it doesn't like having its tail pulled, that it is an individual with feelings.
- A dog needs some control. Controlling another creature will help the child develop self-control.
- A cat or a dog accepts and responds to moods — to loving, to playing, to misery.
- A pet may die. A child will learn the meaning of death, and experience grief.
- Pets reproduce. A child will learn the biological facts of life in a matter-of-fact way.
- Pets need care — to be fed, to be kept clean, to be exercised, to be considered in plans. A child will learn responsibility (within the limits of maturity and capability).
- An animal is an animal. A child will learn and accept the separate natures of, for example, an orphaned wallaby, a kookaburra who calls in for breakfast, a cat stalking a bird, a dog eyeing the guinea pigs.
- Animals can be upset. A child will learn that a pet that is sick or nervous, over-excited, teased, that has its food or plaything removed, or is startled by a sudden approach, may become vicious.

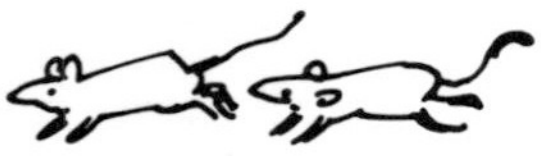

My Dog Spot

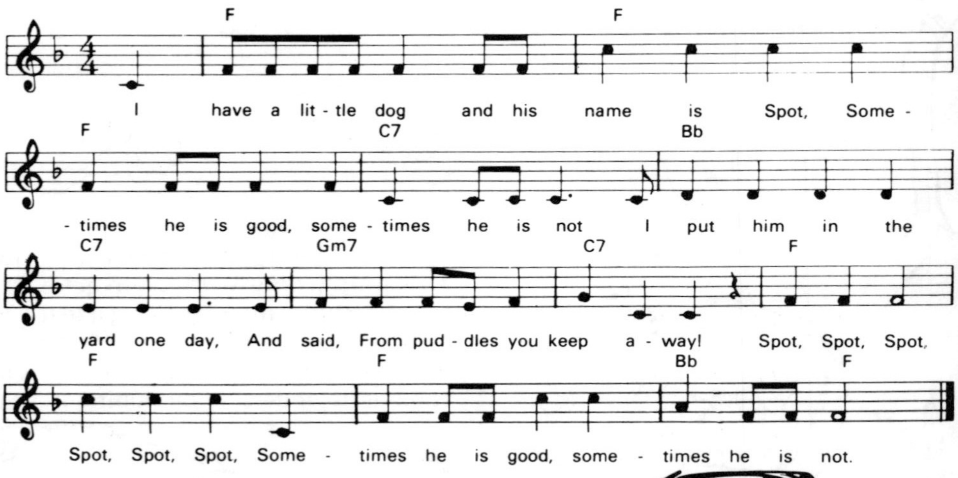

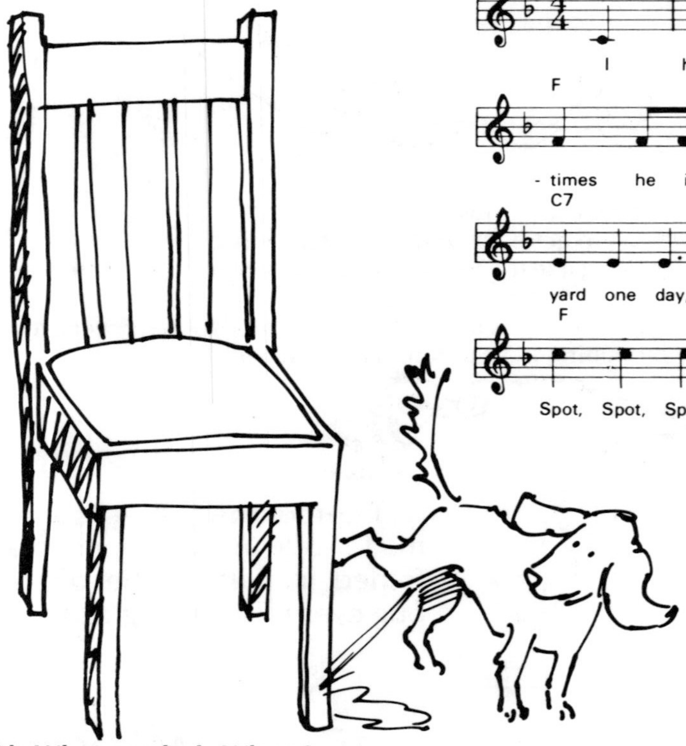

F F
I have a lit - tle dog and his name is Spot, Some -
F C7 Bb
- times he is good, some - times he is not I put him in the
C7 Gm7 C7 F
yard one day, And said, From pud - dles you keep a - way! Spot, Spot, Spot,
F F Bb F
Spot, Spot, Spot, Some - times he is good, some - times he is not.

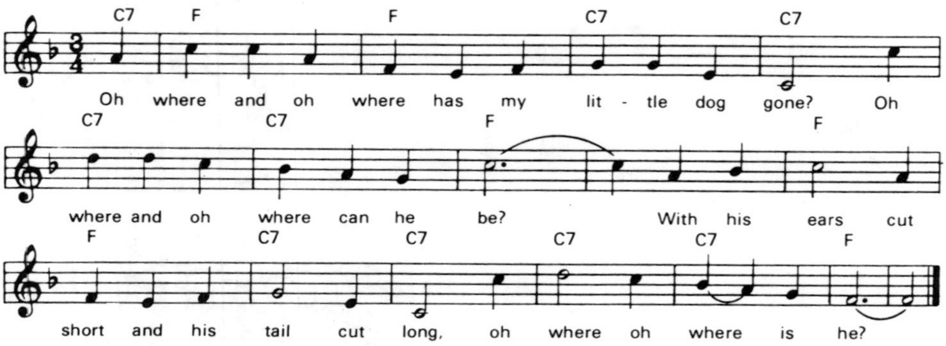

Oh Where and oh Where?

C7 F F C7 C7
Oh where and oh where has my lit - tle dog gone? Oh
C7 C7 F F
where and oh where can he be? With his ears cut
F C7 C7 C7 C7 F
short and his tail cut long, oh where oh where is he?

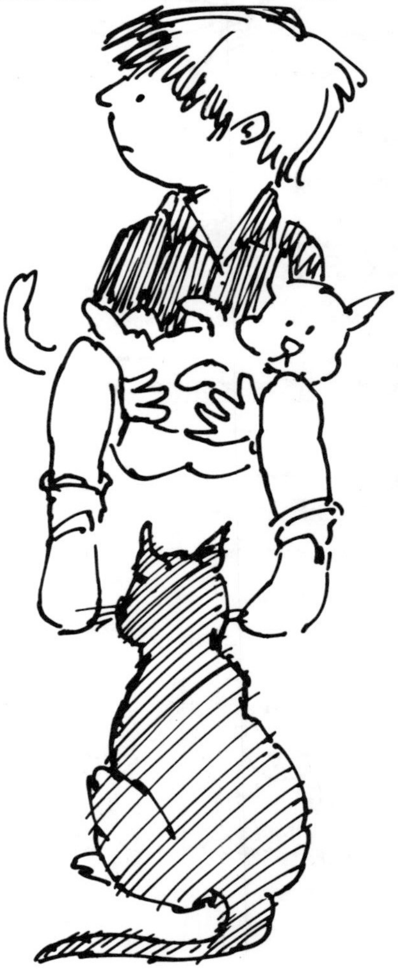

Choosing a Pet

The pet chosen should suit the whole family, so be very realistic about your life habits before you accept the responsibility of a pet. Cats and dogs, guinea pigs, mice, birds and fish are the obvious pets. But have you thought of:

- Silkworms, tadpoles, frogs, caterpillars, snails, beetles, lizards — for city children?
- A poddy lamb, a foal, a duck, or a motherless wallaby — for country children?

Some cats and dogs to make

Pussy Cats Say Miaow

A story to tell as you draw

Once upon a time there was an old woman who lived in a cottage. The cottage had two chimneys on the roof, two windows and a door. One day the old woman went out of the door and along the road to fetch some wood to light her fire. She went up a long winding lane, but there was no wood there. So she went back over to the other side of the road. But the ground was very slippery, and — oops! she fell down. And oops! down again. 'This is no good,' she said to herself, and started walking back along the road. Oops! and oops! down again. She still had found no wood, but she decided to go straight home — and there, beside the cottage door was some firewood! A bundle of sticks on one side of the door, and a bundle of sticks on the other side. So the old woman sat down in front of a warm fire that night — with her pussycat!

Warm Kitty, Soft Kitty

Do you and your child understand the hygiene required for the care and handling of the pet?

MORE ANIMALS

Little Peter Rabbit

Little Peter Rabbit had a cold upon his chest,
Little Peter Rabbit had a cold upon his chest,
Little Peter Rabbit had a cold upon his chest,
So he rubbed it with camphorated oil.

Little Peter Rabbit had a very floppy ear — oh dear,
So he flipped it and he flopped it and it stood up straight.
Little Peter Rabbit had a prickle in his toe — ouch!
So he pulled it and he pulled it, and it came right out.

You can sing this as a 'disappearing' song, dropping one word from the end each time you sing it. Or you can sing it by substituting an action (as above) for each phrase.

Five Little Ducks

Four little ducks . . .
Three little ducks . .
Two little ducks . . .

One little duck went out one day,
Over the hills and far away
Mother duck said, 'Quack, quack, quack, quack!'
And none of those little ducks came back.

Old mother duck went out one day,
Over the hills and far away,
Mother duck said, 'Quack, quack, quack, quack!'
And *all* of the five little ducks came back.

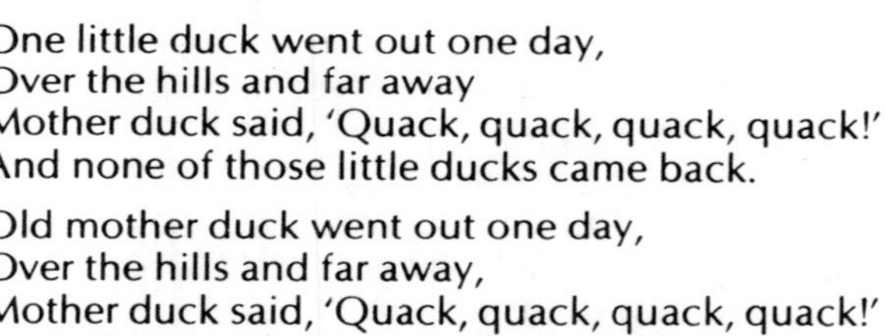

Some animals to make

A little duck can be made out of a matchbox, a pipe cleaner and a bead.

Socks can be made into all sorts of animal puppets. Pull the sock on your hand so that the heel is on your knuckles. Tuck the toe part well into the palm of your hand, then your puppet will have an expressive mouth.
Add features by cutting them out of paper and pasting or stapling them on, sewing on buttons for eyes, embroidering or adding lengths of wool, straw or pipe cleaners for whiskers, etc. Stretch part of the sock and tie or secure with an elastic band — for rabbit's ears, an elephant's trunk, etc.

Ride a Cock Horse

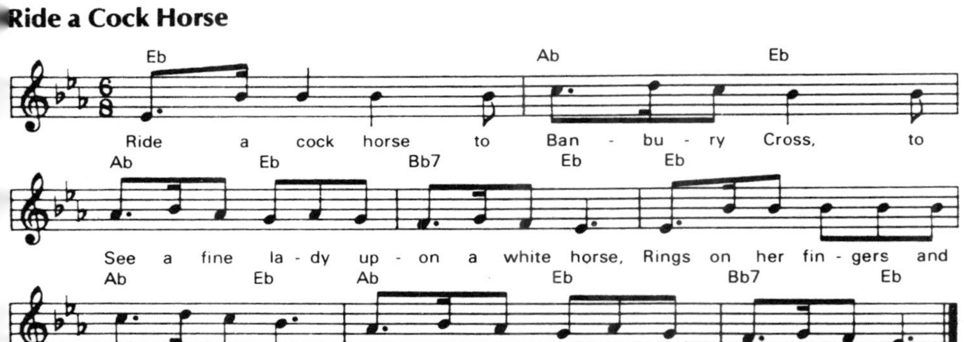

A hobby horse

A hobby horse can be an ordinary broom, or a bought toy – but you could make one with a length of dowel about the height of the child. The head could be:

- A gumboot tied on firmly. Stick on paper eyes, and perhaps give it a mane of shredded paper or wood shavings.
- An old sock, stuffed with newspaper. Ears can be twisted up and held with elastic bands. For a long-lived hobby horse, you could sew on features.

A wooden hobby horse is easy to make from timber offcuts. Choose flat wood instead of dowel and nail on a flat piece of ply that looks vaguely horse-head shaped. The eyes can be metal bottle tops nailed on, the mane some plastic fringing, a cake frill, shredded paper or wood shavings and you can nail a rope around the nose for reins.

If you have an old horseshoe, string it up somewhere so that your child can play it with a long nail, or a metal spoon, like a triangle.

Blocks of timber can be made into clip-clop horses' feet.

Singing a Cowboy Song

This is the Way the Ladies Ride

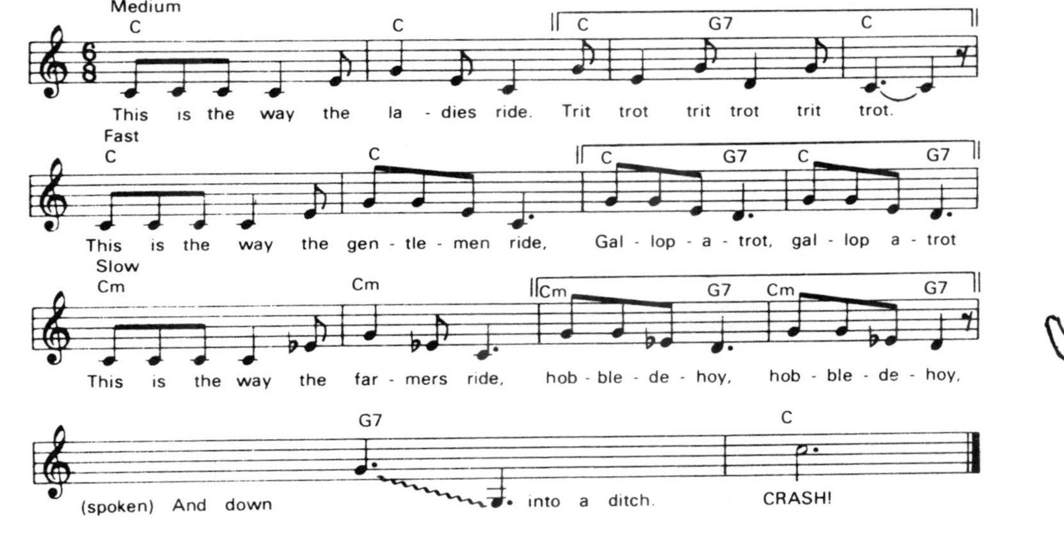

WILD ANIMALS

A Fat Hippopotamus

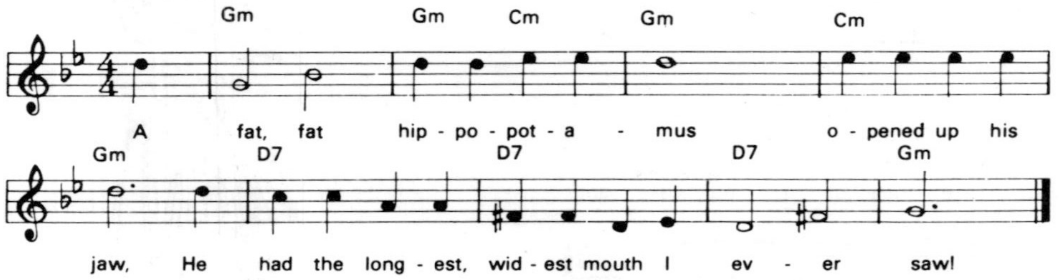

A fat, fat hip-po-pot-a-mus o-pened up his jaw,
He had the long-est, wid-est mouth I ev-er saw!

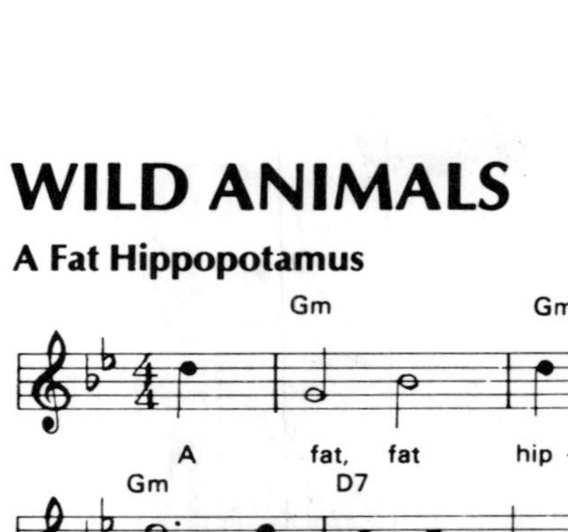

The Elephant Wobbles

The el-e-phant wob-bles from side to side, he's ter-ri-bly big and he's ter-ri-bly wide, and peo-ple shout wher-ev-er he goes "Good-ness gra-cious what a nose!"

The tortoise goes with a slurpity-slop,
If she went much slower, she would stop,
And people shout when they see her go,
'Goodness gracious, aren't you slow!'

The kangaroo goes with a bumpety-bump,
He'll never walk when he can jump,
And people shout to him in the street,
'Goodness gracious, what big feet!'

Look at the Monkey

Look at the monk-ey, sit-ting on the tree!
Looks like he's going to fall on me,
Oh, diddle diddle dum, oh diddle diddle dum.

Look at his tail, all long and thin,
Looks like a snake on the end of him,
Oh, diddle, diddle, dum, oh, diddle, diddle, dum.

Look at him now, he's scratching his nose,
Must be nice not to need some clothes,
Oh, diddle, diddle, dum, oh, diddle, diddle, dum.

The Lion

I'm a big fierce lion
With long sharp claws,
And I'm prowling around
On four soft paws.
With a swish of my tail
And a swipe with my claws,
I'm looking for something
To munch with my jaws! Growl!

Monkey, monkey moo,
Monkey, monkey do,
I'm a monkey,
You're a monkey,
He's a monkey, too!

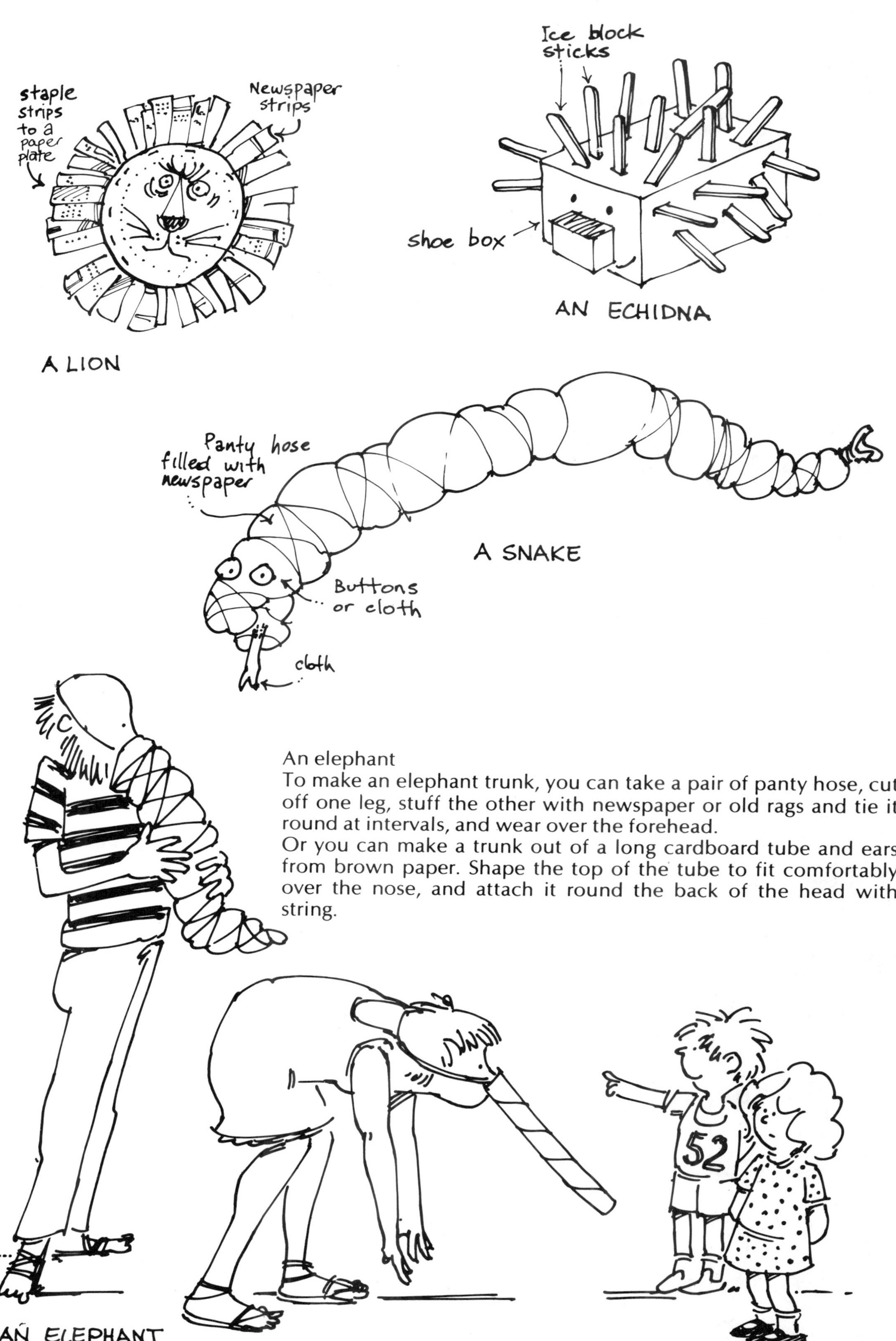

An elephant

To make an elephant trunk, you can take a pair of panty hose, cut off one leg, stuff the other with newspaper or old rags and tie it round at intervals, and wear over the forehead.

Or you can make a trunk out of a long cardboard tube and ears from brown paper. Shape the top of the tube to fit comfortably over the nose, and attach it round the back of the head with string.

SOME TOYS TO MAKE

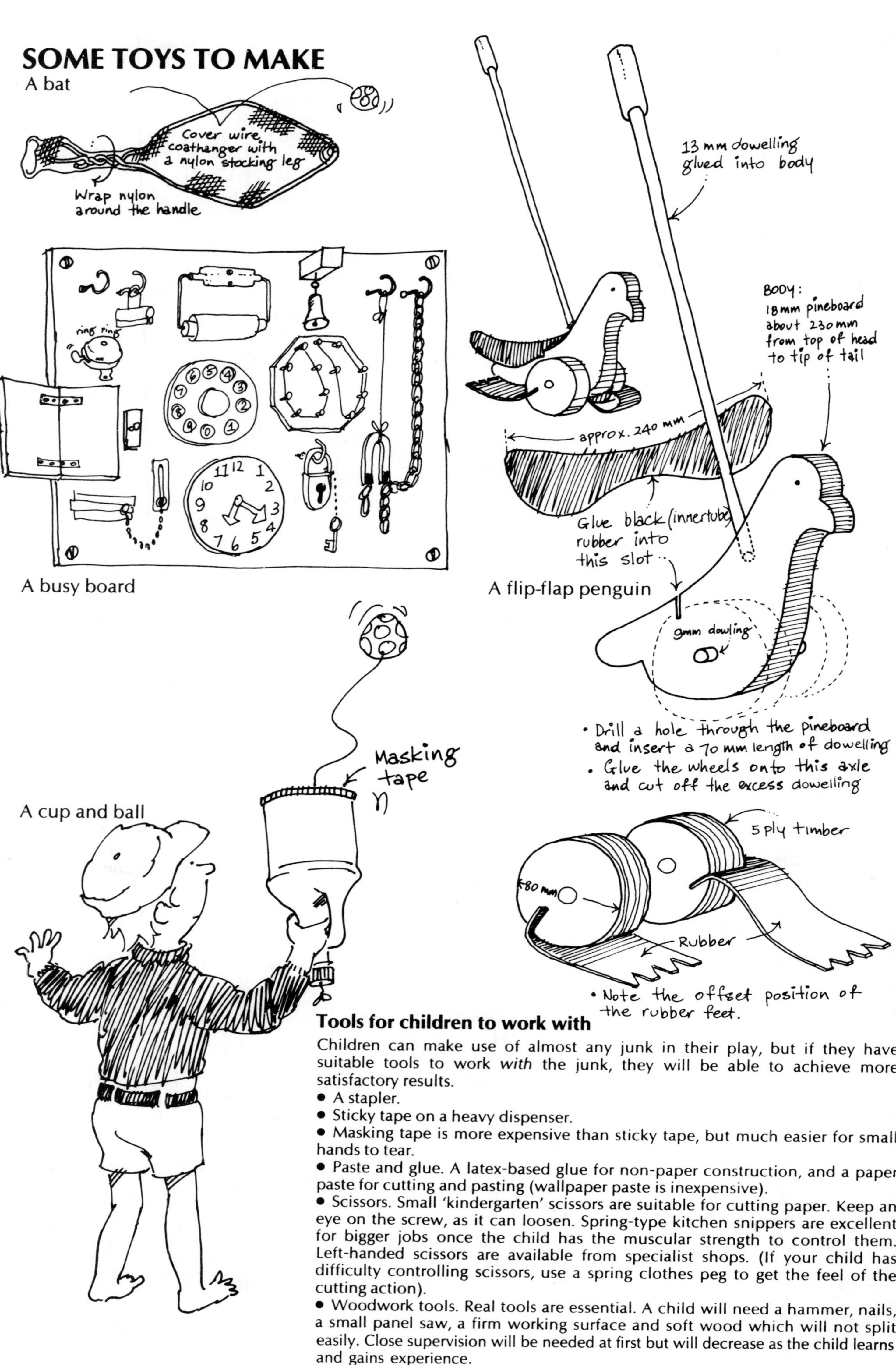

Tools for children to work with

Children can make use of almost any junk in their play, but if they have suitable tools to work *with* the junk, they will be able to achieve more satisfactory results.

- A stapler.
- Sticky tape on a heavy dispenser.
- Masking tape is more expensive than sticky tape, but much easier for small hands to tear.
- Paste and glue. A latex-based glue for non-paper construction, and a paper paste for cutting and pasting (wallpaper paste is inexpensive).
- Scissors. Small 'kindergarten' scissors are suitable for cutting paper. Keep an eye on the screw, as it can loosen. Spring-type kitchen snippers are excellent for bigger jobs once the child has the muscular strength to control them. Left-handed scissors are available from specialist shops. (If your child has difficulty controlling scissors, use a spring clothes peg to get the feel of the cutting action).
- Woodwork tools. Real tools are essential. A child will need a hammer, nails, a small panel saw, a firm working surface and soft wood which will not split easily. Close supervision will be needed at first but will decrease as the child learns and gains experience.

ROBOTS AND MONSTERS

Paper strips, wool, string etc

cotton reels

Wood shavings

steel Wool

Coloured felt

Tennis ball

Draw mouth with felt pen

HEAD Crunched up paper

Screw eyes

Curtain wires

Tin foil

Polystyrene

plastic spoons

Pipe cleaners

A FUNNY PAGE

Boom, Boom, Ain't it Great to be Crazy?

What makes children laugh?

Children laugh at different things at different ages.

- When children have learnt which foot is which, they can laugh at someone putting shoes on the wrong foot.
- When children have learnt basic language, they can enjoy playing with words — 'turkey-lurkey', 'wicky-wocky', etc.
- When children have learnt the norms of physical movement, they will be amused by tripping, slipping and contorting.

So don't be surprised if a very young child is mystified or frightened by things that send the older children into hysterics.

Fooba Wooba John

Heard a cow say miaow, fooba wooba, fooba wooba,
Heard a cow say miaow, fooba wooba John.

Heard a cow say miaow, Then I heard it say bow-wow,
Hey John, ho John, fooba wooba John.

Make up new verses. Rhymes are not really required. The only rule is to keep it silly.

Mixed-up Nursery Rhymes

Try mixing up the words of nursery rhymes your child knows well. For example:

Humpty Dumpty sat on a bumble,
Humpty Dumpty had a big tumble,
All the King's horses and all the King's men,
Couldn't put Humpty together again.

Hickory Dickory Dock,
A frog jumped into my sock . . .

Polly put the telly on . . .

Riddles

The verbal understanding to cope with riddles probably doesn't come until about the age of five or six, but here are some old chestnuts.

A horse goes on four feet, a man on two feet, what goes on one foot? *A sock.*
What do you call an elephant that flies? *A jumbo jet.*
What sort of pie has feathers and can fly? *A magpie.*
What always goes to sleep with its shoes on? *A horse.*
What sort of dog is long and round and red and you find it inside a bread roll? *A hot dog.*
Why does a rabbit have a shiny nose? *Because its powder puff is at the other end.*
What is the biggest mouse in all the world? *A hippopota-mouse.*

Some Silly Songs

Nicholas Ned

What else could Nicholas put on his head? A carrot? A tractor? An ice-cream?

Pop! Goes the Weasel

Suzy Had a Baby

Mumps, said the doctor, measles said the nurse,
Chicken pox, said the lady with the alligator purse,
Out went the doctor, out went the nurse,
Out went the lady with the alligator purse.

GOING OUT – NEAR HOME

A young child will enjoy the most mundane of expeditions, provided you give your time and attention. Follow the child's pace, notice what seems to be interesting, talk about what you're seeing. To follow up the trip, leave out playthings that relate to what you've done.

What Shall We Do When We All Go Out?

Make up verses to suit your outing, e.g., 'We'll see the ducks when we all go out . . . '

Interesting trips with a young child

At Home

- Go on a special discovery walk around your house. Look at precious ornaments, your jewels, photographs, silver that's put away for best, old picture books. Look for things made of wood, things made of glass, blue things, smooth or rough things.
- Go out into the yard with a big magnifying glass. Look at leaves, bark, ants, a caterpillar.
- Take a picnic out into the back yard (or have an indoor picnic on a wet day).

The Local Shops

- Watch the refrigerated truck delivering meat to the butcher. Some butchers might let you go round the back to see them make the sausages.
- Watch the local greengrocer counting oranges or weighing beans and putting them in bags, or the florist making up bouquets.
- If there's a small restaurant, they might let you see the kitchen. For a special treat, sit at a table and be waited on.
- Watch the shoe mender at work, or the pizza maker.
- Perhaps there's a pet shop. Pet shop owners usually don't mind children looking around.
- What's going on at the local garage? Is there a car wash?
- Is there a shop with an escalator or a lift?
- It's fascinating to watch timber being sawn. Is there a timber yard nearby or a hardware shop selling timber? Perhaps there are some offcuts, wood shavings or sawdust to take home to work with.

Around the Neighbourhood

- Is there a friendly horse in a paddock or a cocky on a verandah to say hullo to?
- Note when the local letter box is due to be emptied. Go at that time, and watch the post office person taking the letters away.
- Stand outside the local school at playtime and watch the big children and the teachers.
- Is there somewhere to watch trains and wave? Or a bridge to see cars and buses and trucks going underneath?
- Is there any road work going on? Children love to watch bulldozers and graders, front-end loaders and tip trucks; people telling the traffic to stop and go, or people digging with picks or jackhammers. Look inside the little huts where they keep their tools and make their tea.
- Is there any building going on? Everything about building is fascinating – the wrecking, the digging, cranes, hammers or painting.
- Maybe someone is moving house, or goods are being delivered somewhere. Stand and watch as people load or unload the truck.
- Take out a picnic to a nearby park, or a paddock. Eating is much more interesting outside.

Talk about what you see. If you cannot find time to discuss interesting discoveries, your child will grow to have little belief in the value of observations.

Running to the Corner
Run - ning to the corn - er, run - ning ver - y fast, Run - ning to the
corn - er, get - ting there at last, I'm puff, puff, puff, puff, puf - fing, I'm
puf - fing a lot, I'm hot, hot, hot!
Run - ning from the corn - er, run back home a - gain, Run - ning from the
corn - er, run - ning back and then, I'm puff, puff, puff, puff, puf - fing, I'm
puf - fing a lot, I'm hot, hot, hot!
Stop, Look and Listen
When we want to cross the road, There are things we al - ways
do And I'll tell you what they are So that you can do them
too. Well, we stop! (Yes, we stop.) And we look! (Yes, we
look.) And we lis - ten! (Yes, we lis - ten.)
What for? For the cars, honk, honk, And the
bus - es, beep beep, And the bikes, ting - a - ling - a-ling - a -
ling! That's why we stop! Yes, we stop! And we look! Yes, we
look! And we lis - ten. Noth - ing com-ing? Then we go.
Judgment of distance and danger are learnt by experience. It's hard for a young child to cross a road alone. The child should: hold a grown-up's hand; go to a traffic control, e.g., a marked crossing, the lights, a police officer, a lollipop lady. Always be safety conscious yourself.

GOING SHOPPING

Going Shopping with a Child

An outing doesn't have to be 'special' to provide a learning experience, provided you recognise that the child has an equal interest in it, a desire to be heard, to be involved, to be considered. As with your household activities, the ordinary shopping trip can be a valuable learning time for a young child.

- Before you go, you could involve the child in your list-making, perhaps by remembering things for you. You could 'draw' your list, or cut out pictures from magazines. Decide which shops you're going to. Perhaps plan for an ice cream when you've done everything.
- At a supermarket, a child could help you find items. That gives practice in:
  relating names to objects, e.g., what is 'salami' or 'cheese'?
  recognising categories, e.g., 'cereals', 'frozen foods'
  'reading' pictures on labels, e.g., 'strawberry' or 'apricot' yoghurt.

(With a bit of practice, the child will probably know what's on those bewildering shelves better than you do!)

The shopping situation is a fruitful one for exploring what behaviour you will accept from each other. Are you going to give in, snap or be firm if the child whinges? If you get cranky because you can't find anyone to help you, the bottom falls out of the supermarket bag or the baby starts yelling, how will the child react? People learn acceptable behaviour by trial and error, and you both need practice to understand and set the limits.

Five Currant Buns

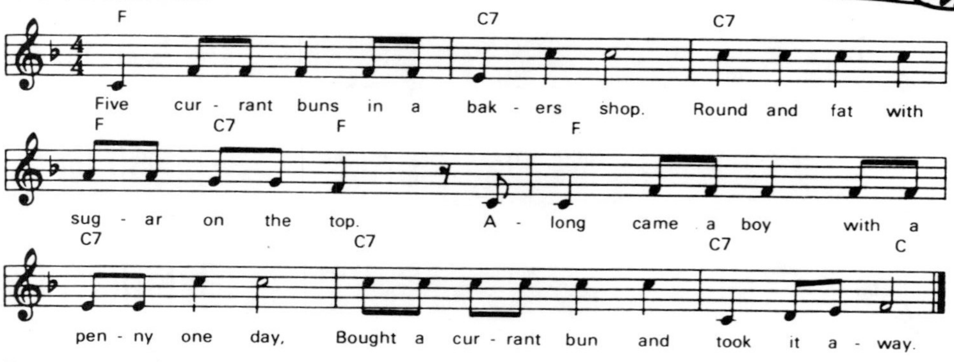

Four currant buns . . . etc.

Playing Shops

Playing shops involves the child in useful verbal interaction, clear role taking, and opportunities for practising mathematics. It can be anything from a simple imaginative game involving nothing at all, to an elaborate one involving setting up a shop.

Some shop ideas (but the child's imagination will outstrip yours):

Display containers
- shoeboxes or lids
- the polystyrene trays from the butcher or greengrocer
- the flat parts of egg cartons

A cake shop
- egg cartons (the bumpy part) for buns or scones - currant ones can have dots drawn on
- shoe boxes for bread
- short cardboard rolls for finger buns or swiss rolls
- play-dough cakes and biscuits
- bathroom 'sponge' cakes and 'rock' cakes

A fruit shop
- scrunched-up newspaper for lettuces and cabbages
- tennis ball oranges
- cardboard roll cucumbers and zucchinis
- stones for potatoes
- fir cones for pears or turnips
- pebbles for berry fruit

A butcher
- cardboard roll sausages

A supermarket
- empty packets, plastic bottles, tins with lids

A shoe shop
- a selection of the family's shoes
- (ask for them to be put away afterwards)

A chemist
- tissue boxes, old lipsticks, shampoo bottles

Money
- can be shells, leaves, gumnuts, milk bottle tops . . . or you can provide say, 20 cents worth of small change to give an understanding of real money.

Eat Brown Bread

C C Am
I - tidd - ly - i - ti, Eat brown bread, I saw a saus - age
G7 C C C7
Fall down dead. Up jumped a sav - el - oy And
F D7 G7 C G7 C
bashed him on the head. I - tidd - ly - i - ti, BROWN BREAD.

WHEN YOU GO OUT

Waiting Rooms

You may have to sit around in a waiting room if you go to the hospital, the clinic, the doctor or the dentist, and waiting rooms, even if they're supplied with children's books and toys, can be very boring for a child.
Take a treasure bag (as for a car journey, p.71).
Use the time to sing songs, play games, tell stories – quietly. The rest of the patients will probably enjoy the display much more than if you were fighting a losing battle to keep the child sitting silently on a chair.
(If you're making a routine visit to the doctor or dentist, you could take the child in with you to get used to it. It may save tears and fears later.)

Friends and Relations

Other people's houses aren't always equipped to entertain your child.

- Glance swiftly around for sources of danger or embarrassment – open fires, low ornaments, etc.
- Take the ubiquitous treasure bag.
- Work out a fair bargain about the amount of attention the child can expect from you. A child may get jealous if left out of conversations.

When you go out without your child

- Do not leave the child at home alone. If possible, find a babysitter known to both you and your child. If not, make time on the first occasion to get them both acquainted.
- Leave a clear set of instructions for the babysitter, including where you may be contacted. Leave emergency numbers near the telephone.
- Tell the child you are going out.

It is courtesy to the babysitter for the parents to:

- Say when they expect to be home and ring up if they are likely to be much later (a school student who has to be up in the morning could perhaps sleep the night).
- Establish the going rate and pay it.
- Leave out something for the babysitter to eat and drink.
- Get the babysitter home safely.
- Tell the babysitter if there is any special terminology the child uses e.g., for going to the toilet.
- Make the house rules clear. Children may try to bluff the babysitter.

Suggestions for the babysitter
Be sure the parents give you full instructions and follow them carefully.
In case of sudden illness or accident phone them for advice.
If they are going to be unavailable, have them nominate someone else you can contact.

In case of fire or smoke:
Get the children out of the house immediately, without stopping to dress them or to make a telephone call. Take the children to the nearest neighbour, then call the fire department first, then the parents second.

Do not open the door to strangers.
If you cannot identify a sound, call the police, then the parents.
Never leave the children in the house alone, even for a minute. If a child awakens crying but does not feel feverish, tender loving care will usually help. If all fails, call the parents.
Remember that your primary job is to care for the children.

When you go out to work

If you go to work and you leave your child in someone's care, you may feel guilty. Perhaps you bribe your child not to cry when you leave, or you buy special presents when you come home from work. The message you're then giving the child is that being minded is nasty and that there will be a special treat for tolerating it.

It's not a sin to leave a child in someone's care. Just be sure that when you are with the child, you make the most of your time together.

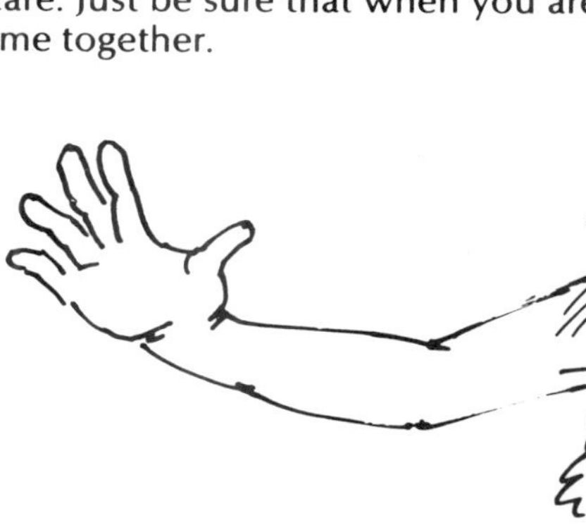

Choosing a minding situation

Be aware of the different situations available to you and choose one that suits your circumstances and lifestyle. It's unfair to keep moving a young child, so choose carefully. If you're not happy with the situation, your child is likely to be unhappy in it too. You might consider:

- Family day care.
- Long day care centres.
- Pre-schools.
- Neighbourhood children's centres.
- Occasional care centres.

For information about the services in your state, consult the authorities listed on page 79.

Points to look for:

- Is the service registered? If so, is it supervised regularly?
- Is it safe? Are there safety fences and gates with latches that work?
- Is it well-ventilated and clean?
- Is the play area safe, with space for boisterous as well as quiet play?
- Is there plenty for the children to do?
- Are the grown-ups involved with the children?
- How does the place feel? Relaxed or rushed? Do you and your child feel welcome?

Take the child with you to look at the situation. You can sense through your child whether someone is a genuinely sympathetic person.

Hellos and Goodbyes

- Leave the child suitably dressed (children are likely to get messy) and with extra clothes for weather changes and accidents.
- Make sure you can be contacted.
- Stay around to ease the transition, but not for too long. Interest the child in something, and when you leave tell the child you're doing so and when you'll be back. If the child does cry, chances are the tears will stop as soon as you're out of sight.
- It sometimes helps to leave the child with something of yours to mind, e.g., a scarf or something from your bag, as a pledge of your return.
- Collect the child at the appointed time or give reasonable notice of a change.
- Show an interest in what the child has been doing. A remark such as, 'That shirt's *covered* in paint' could imply criticism.
- Try to allow time to share with the staff the happenings of the day or night. A care-giver would like to know, for example, if a child has been awake half the night. She might have been planning a visit to the zoo.

GOING ON AN OUTING

Planning a trip

- Try not to do too much. Maybe a young child is happier seeing four or five animals at the zoo and going home than 'doing' the whole place. If you're in a hurry and you rush round yanking the child everywhere, the trip will be spoiled.
- If a long journey is involved, or there is likely to be waiting time, let the child take a special bag with a favourite toy and some bits and pieces.
- Do you usually take extra clothes — a jumper, spare pants, a clean shirt — and some food and drink? It's probably healthier and cheaper than what you would buy, and you can still buy a treat.
- Try to be comfortable physically. If you're carrying too much and your feet hurt, you won't enjoy yourself, and if you don't, other people won't either.
- Never pass by a clean toilet!
- The ideal is to allow one person per child. High school children are often happy to accompany you on interesting trips, and relate well to pre-schoolers.
- Discuss what to do if someone gets lost. You could pin the children's names, addresses and phone numbers *inside* their clothing, telling them what it is (as with 'name' T-shirts, one doesn't like the thought of a stranger noticing a child's name and using it to entice the child away).

Let's Go to the Zoo

Let's go to the zoo and see the roaring lion,
Let's go to the zoo and see the roaring lion,
The lion he walks around like this, *etc.*

Let's go to the zoo and see the big grey elephant, *etc.*
The elephant, he swings his trunk like this, *etc.*

Let's go to the zoo and see the big tall giraffe, *etc.*
The giraffe, she holds her head so high, *etc.*

Let's go to the zoo and see the slippery snake, *etc.*
The snake, he slithers here and there, *etc.*

Let's go to the zoo and see the kangaroo, *etc.*
The kangaroo, she hops like this, *etc.*

Let's go to the zoo and see the monkeys climb, *etc.*
The monkeys, they climb from here to there, *etc.*

Let's go to the zoo and see the grizzly bear, *etc.*
The bear, he goes into his cave, *etc.*

Some Places to Go

The Airport
Big jets . . . little planes . . . helicopters . . . escalators . . . baggage collection . . . airports are fascinating places.

Zoos and Animal Parks
Most of these make special provision for young children, and there are tame animals to feed and touch.

A Farm
Australian farms are not usually of the 'Old Macdonald' variety, but you can sometimes find a farm geared to show children around.

The Fire Station
If you want to see round properly, make an appointment and go in a group. Firefighters are traditionally friendly to small children, but they have a job to do. Children may need to be four years old or more.

The Show
Again, don't try to 'do' everything. If possible plan your time so that you're at the right place at the right time, but be responsive to interests the child develops.

I Went to Visit a Farm

IN THE CAR

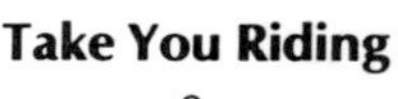

Take You Riding

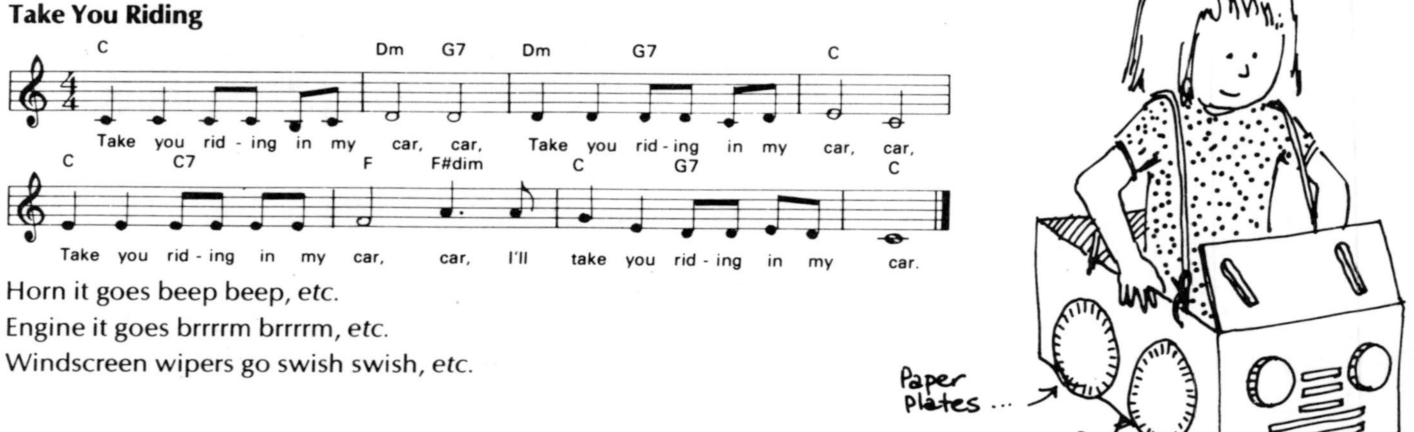

Horn it goes beep beep, *etc.*
Engine it goes brrrrm brrrrm, *etc.*
Windscreen wipers go swish swish, *etc.*

Children are active beings. They don't naturally spend hours (or even minutes) sitting passively on a chair, unless perhaps they're watching television — yet that's what they're expected to do in a car.

Some ways to make car trips tolerable

- Allow time to stop frequently so that children can run about. Babies can be taken out and allowed to lie on their stomachs, or kick for a few minutes.
- Make sure the car is comfortable with pillows and blankets.
- Have non-messy food and drinks easily accessible. Plastic drinking mugs with spouts prevent spills in a car.
- On a long trip, the camping site near a natural local attraction may be more interesting than the television set in a motel.
- Have a portable cooler for food and extra drink in case of vehicle breakdown in country areas.
- A child who
  can see out well
  hasn't just eaten a big meal, or drunk a milkshake
  sucks a barley sugar

is less likely to be carsick, providing no one suggests the possibility.

But be prepared!

This Old Man

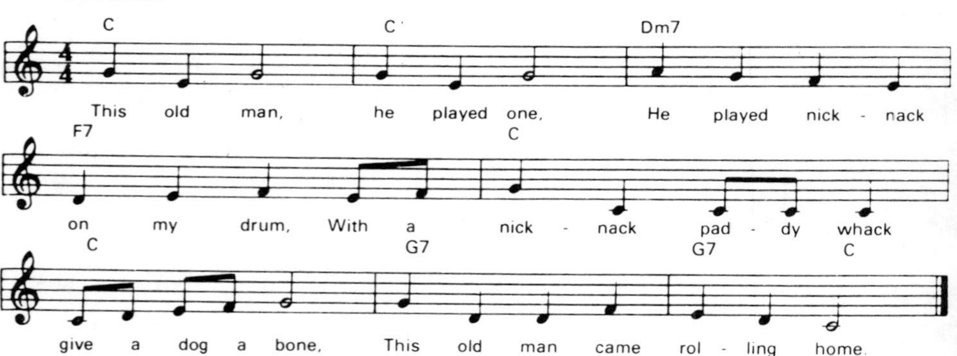

This old man, he played two,
He played nick nack on my shoe,
Nick nack, *etc.*

This old man, he played three,
He played nick nack on my tree,
Nick nack, *etc.*

This old man, he played four,
He played nick nack on my door,
Nick nack, *etc.*

This old man, he played five,
He played nick nack on my hive,
Nick nack, *etc.*

This old man, he played six,
He played nick nack on my sticks,
Nick nack, *etc.*

This old man, he played seven,
He played nick nack down in Devon
Nick nack, *etc.*

This old man, he played eight,
He played nick nack on my gate,
Nick nack, *etc.*

This old man, he played nine,
He played nick nack on my line,
Nick nack, *etc.*

This old man, he played ten,
He played nick nack on my hen,
Nick nack, *etc.*

When taking children in cars:
Strap them in approved safety seats or belts — always.
Don't strap two children in together and never nurse a child in the front seat.
Don't leave a baby or child alone in a car.
An angry driver is a dangerous driver. If something happens to upset you, stop the car.

Ideas for Car Trips

- You can buy moulded cushions so that the child can see out more easily.
- Involve the child in the journey. Change places so the child can sit in the front sometimes (with an approved restraint) to help watch for traffic lights and road signs.

What can you see? How many? What colour?

Things for a car 'treasure bag'

- Crayons (better than pencils, which poke when jolted).
- Paper, on a pad or notebook with reasonably firm backing to press on.
- Toys — matchbox cars, dolls with extra clothes, magnetic board games, magic writing or drawing sets, cards, toys that haven't been seen for a while.
- A packet of pipe cleaners to make people, spiders, spectacles or long chains.
- Wool to do cat's cradle, french knitting, or just wind round things.
- Playdough or plasticene and a small board.
- Individual food supplies — little containers of dried fruit, chewing gum, little cereal packs.
- Cassettes of favourite songs, stories and music.
- A litter bag.

Scissors Stone Paper

Things to do

- Take the opportunity to reminisce about your own childhood or your child's baby days.
- Make up part of a story. Pass it on to the next person to continue.
- Play hand games such as scissors, stone and paper. On the count of three, each player presents a hand in the form of scissors, stone or paper:
  stone beats scissors — it blunts them
  paper beats stone — it wraps it
  scissors beat paper — they cut it.
- Do mini-hand mimes — demonstrate an action for someone else to guess, using your hands only.

Scissors beat paper

Games after dark

Noises — one person makes a noise and the others have to guess what the noise represents.

What's This? — put an object in a handkerchief or a thin bag and pass it to somebody to guess what it is by feeling it.

Singing games

A concert — each occupant of the car takes turns to sing a song or tell a story, joke or rhyme.

Make up nonsense versions of known songs — e.g., 'Woof woof, black sheep, have you any pies?'

Sing *long* songs.

Observation Games

Your child may not be able to play the traditional 'I Spy' game, 'I spy with my little eye, something beginning with B. . .' but you can adapt it. You could use a colour, for example, 'I spy with my little eye, something blue . . .' or a brief description, 'I spy with my little eye, something with eight wheels . . .' or a sound equivalent, 'I spy with my little eye, something that sounds like knee. It has green leaves. It's a tree.' Remember that all those playing the game must be able to see the object being guessed. You could give individual children their own list of things to watch for — draw the objects if they cannot read. They could mark off what they have seen.

Score points for seeing various objects e.g., cows, people on bicycles, etc. Make up the rules to suit your family's degree of competitiveness.

TRUCKS AND BUSES, TRAINS AND PLANES

The Little Red Wagon

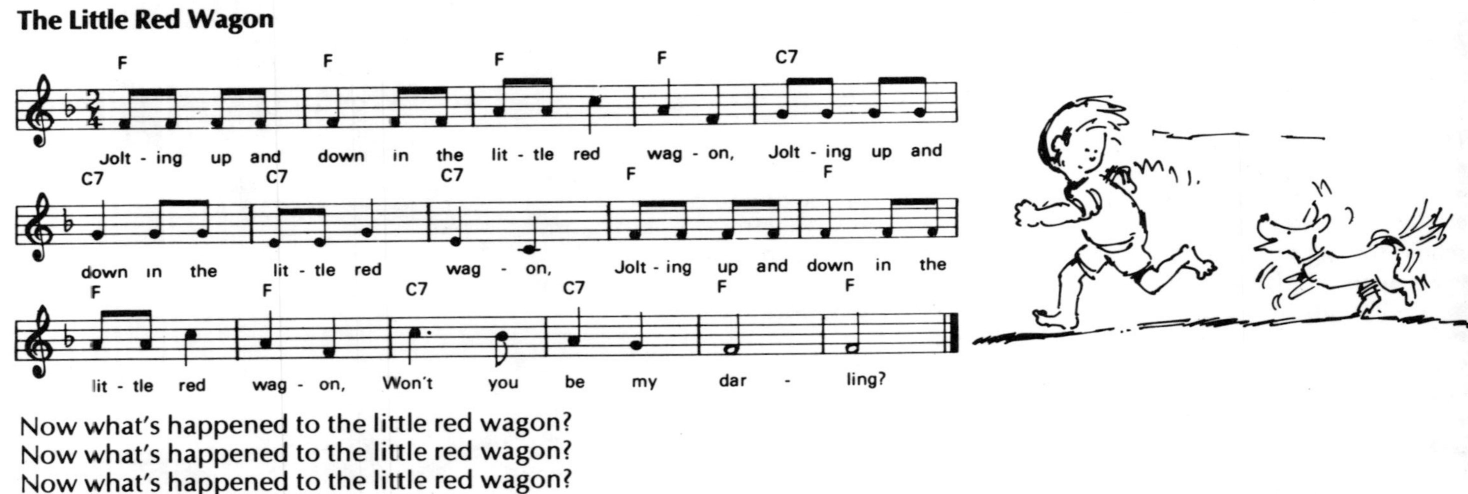

Now what's happened to the little red wagon?
Now what's happened to the little red wagon?
Now what's happened to the little red wagon?
Won't you be my darling?

One wheel's off and the axle's dragging, *etc.*

Let's get a hammer and we can fix it, *etc.*

A Squeaky Old Truck

Train is A-Coming

The Wheels of the Bus

The horn on the bus goes peep, peep, peep, *etc.*
The kids on the bus go wriggle, wriggle, wriggle, *etc.*
The babies on the bus go waa, waa, waa, *etc.*
The windscreen wipers go swish, swish, swish, *etc.*
The people on the bus bounce up and down, *etc.*

I'd Like to Drive a Big Blue Bus

Zoom

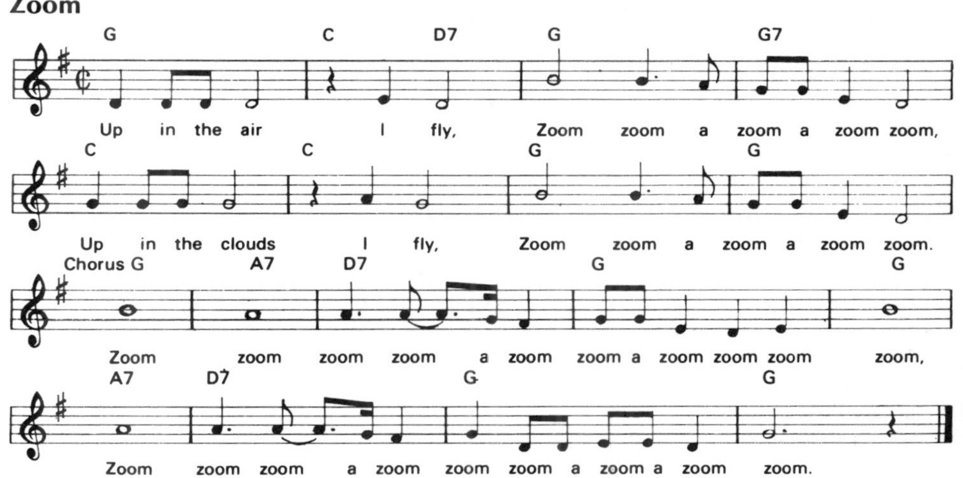

Boxes make good cars. Wheels can be cotton reels, sticky tape cores, typewriter spools, circular lids or paper plates.

A little Plane

Making Big and Little Vehicles

Big vehicles can be made with fruit boxes and cartons.
For a train, link them together with rope or string.
Garbage can lids or old tyres can be wheels.
A plank can be the wings of a plane.
An old pram wheel makes a good steering wheel, or you can push a large paper plate over the end of a broomstick.
Chairs, stools and cushions are useful building materials.

You can make a little plane by just sticking together two iceblock sticks, or by sticking a coathanger onto a long box (e.g. one used for foil).

A little train can be made by pushing matchboxes together, or by linking them with paper slides or pegs.

Some packages have clear cellophane 'windows' which can be used for vehicles, houses, etc.

THE BEACH

Going to the Beach

Sometimes children are frightened of going to the beach. They may be afraid of being separated from you. Sit near a landmark, and discuss where you are. If there are lifesavers around, point them out and tell the children to go to one if they get lost, but try not to let them out of your sight. Children may be afraid of the noise and motion of the waves. You could help a child dig out a 'pool' near the edge of the water. The child will let you know when he or she is ready to brave the surf. Hold the child in your arms as you paddle until confidence grows.

Sand and Water

Sand and water provide infinitely variable learning materials in a situation which naturally attracts a young child.

- There is no right and wrong with sand and water, no success or failure. The child sets the tasks, adapts them in response to the behaviour of the materials, and becomes competent (which in turn develops confidence) without pressure.
- Looking, feeling, tasting and manipulating the materials makes it possible to learn their properties and what can be done with them.
- A child is developing manual intelligence — thinking through the hands. Sand and water present practical problems to solve.
- Sand and water draw children together. A child learns to develop relationships with others, first to play near and watch other children, then to collaborate and share.
- Sand and water provide a useful way of releasing feelings. Digging, pouring water, slapping the sides of a sandcastle and stomping on it when the game is over provide satisfying outlets for tension.

Things to Take to the Beach

- A hat.
- Sunburn cream or lotion.
- A shirt to put on and a sun umbrella if the child burns easily.
- Shoes or sandals. Pavements get hot and there are often broken glass and sharp tins around.
- Something for the child to drink.
- Equipment for playing with sand and water — old spoons, a plastic ice cream container, a bucket, etc.

Some Beach Rules for Children

- Do not throw sand near people. It could get in their eyes.
- Tell the person you're with when you go in swimming.
- Put your rubbish in a bin.

Obey safety rules yourself.
Never allow young children to go to the beach unless they are accompanied by a responsible older person.
Watch your child all the time. Other people may not realise when your child is in difficulties.

Some Beach Ideas

- Someone could draw a line with a stick. Follow the line wherever it goes.
- Burying limbs is fun. (But *not* burying people!)
- Spread out a towel (preferably a plain dark one) and make a picture on it using sprinkles of sand and beach debris.
- Play 'buried treasure'. Bury something in a defined area and smooth over the sand. The children poke sticks where they think the treasure may be. The child with the stick nearest the treasure wins. A younger child will just enjoy digging for it. (Do not forget where you buried the treasure!)

Three Jellyfish

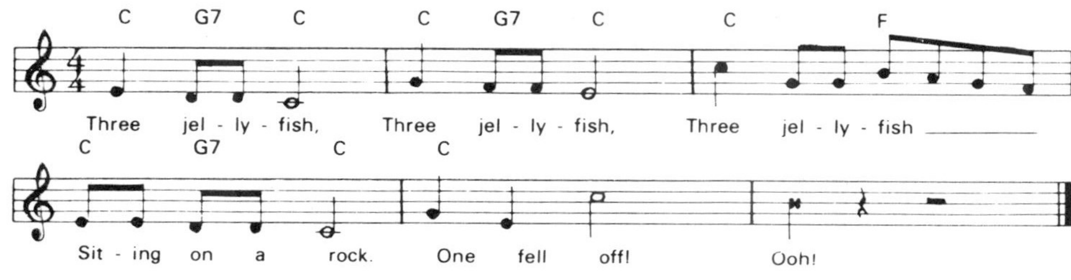

Two jellyfish, two jellyfish, *etc.*
One jellyfish, one jellyfish, *etc.*
No jellyfish, no jellyfish, *etc.*
One jumped on . . . hooray!
One jellyfish, one jellyfish, *etc.*
Another jumped on . . . hooray!
Two jellyfish, two jellyfish, *etc.*
Another jumped on . . . hooray!
Three jellyfish, three jellyfish, *etc.*

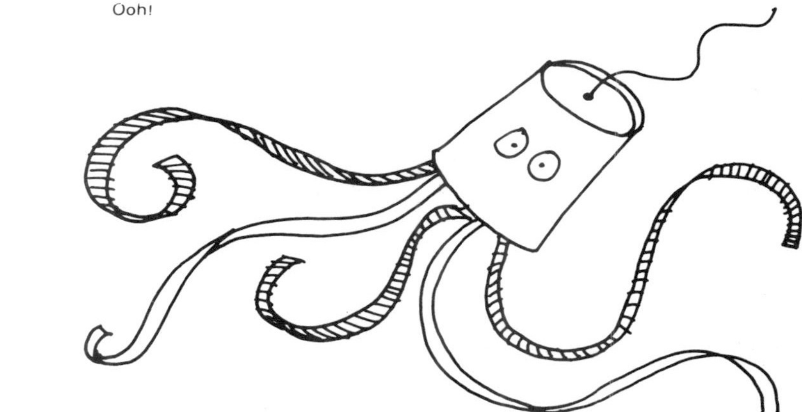

Jellyfish

You can make jellyfish by sticking paper streamers on mousse or little ice cream containers, and a huge octopus can be made with four pairs of old panty hose. Stuff the legs with scrunched-up newspaper, push the tops into one, and fill out with newspaper. Secure with string. You can paint it, add eyes and hang it up.

Collecting Shells

If your child wants to collect some shells, help to check whether there are creatures inside. Shells lose their lustre away from the water. If you want to keep them for something special, you can varnish them.

A child will enjoy having shells just to look at and handle, but here are some ideas for using shells.

- A really nice shell with a hole in it can be threaded onto a leather thong or piece of string or strong cotton for a necklace.
- Shells can be used for play money. (Shells are currency in some parts of the world.)
- Shells can be stuck on boxes. Use a latex glue which dries clear, and varnish when dry.
- 'Beach' pictures can be made with shells and other beach debris. The top of a shoe box lined with dark coloured paper makes a good base. Stick on the shells etc. then squiggle the glue around. Sprinkle on sand. The sand will adhere only to the glue squiggles. A little calendar could be hung on the bottom to make a useful present.

Listen to 'the sound of the sea' in a big shell.

Little Shell

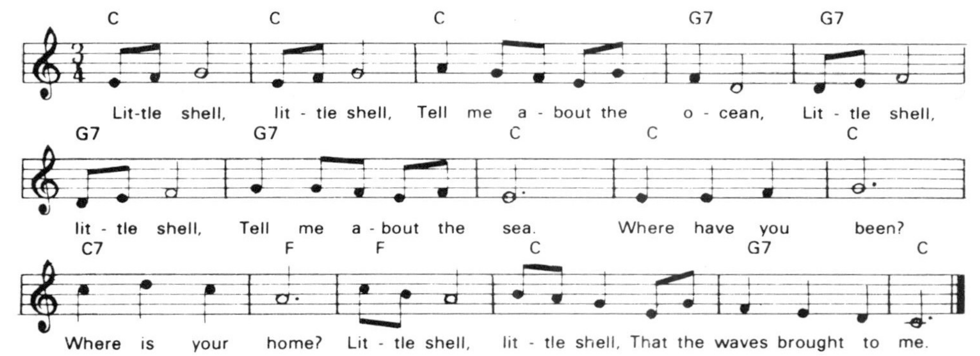

Where have you been?
Where is your home?
Little shell, little shell,
That the waves brought to me.

All sea creatures need to be identified before they're touched — especially a jellyfish or an octopus.

FISH AND BOATS

All the Fish

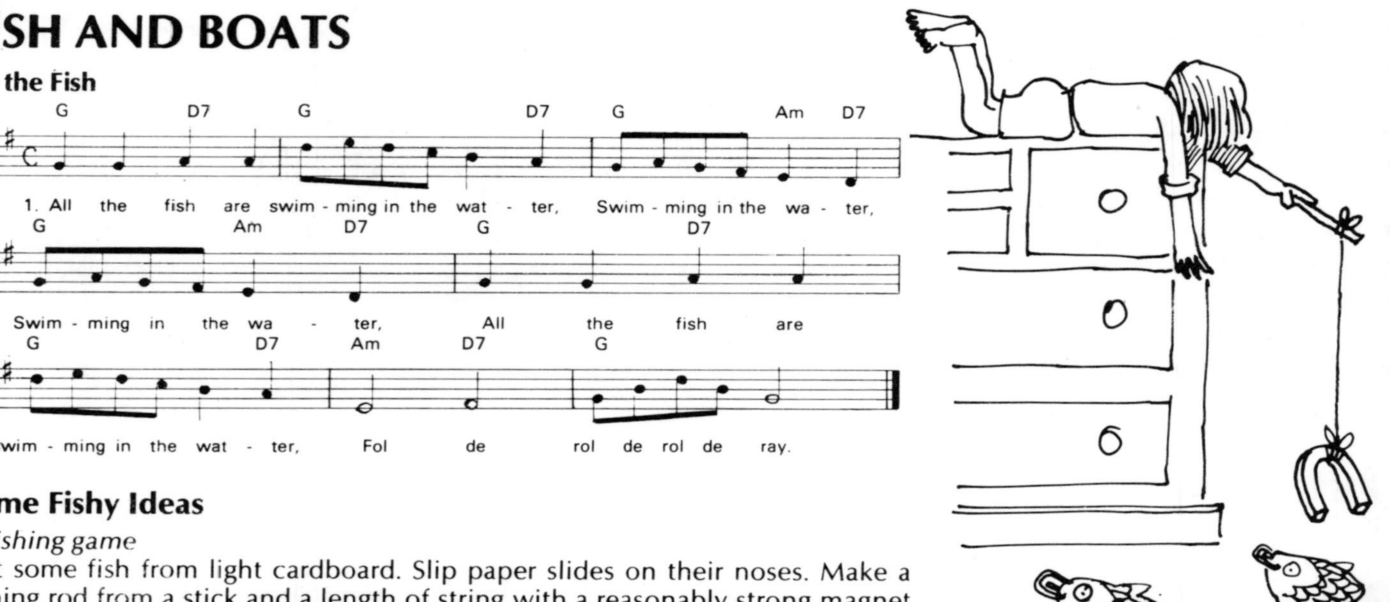

Some Fishy Ideas

A fishing game

Cut some fish from light cardboard. Slip paper slides on their noses. Make a fishing rod from a stick and a length of string with a reasonably strong magnet on the end. Good fishing! (What else will stick to the magnet?)

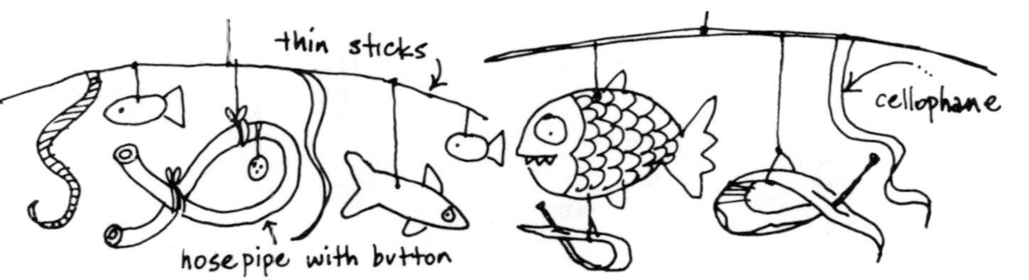

A fish mobile

Fish look good on mobiles because they appear to swim. You can cut them out of cardboard or coloured cellophane paper, or just loop a narrow leaf back on itself and thread the stalk through a little slit, or you can tie a piece of flexible cane or bamboo into a fish shape.

If you're not in a position to keep any other animal, goldfish make undemanding, inexpensive pets. They need minimal care — a tank, tap water, some weed, a *little* pinch of food. Consult a pet shop for details. If the fish dies, why don't you give it a burial in a matchbox in the garden? Recognition of death sharpens a child's appreciation of the value of life.

One, Two, Three, Four, Five

Wherever there is water, never leave a child.

Why did you let it go?
Because it bit my finger so.
Which finger did it bite?
The little finger on the right.

Never dive into shallow water. Spinal injuries can be forever.

When your child needs to know left from right, a felt pen dot on the right hand may help. Being left-handed is no problem, but problems can come if attempts are made to force a change.

Things To Do By a River

- River beds are fascinating fossicking grounds. You can find interesting pebbles, semi-precious stones, old bottles, things swept downstream from miles away, and sometimes even *gold*.
- You can play Pooh Sticks (a game invented by Winnie-the-Pooh). Stand on a bridge and drop sticks in the upstream side. Hurry across to the other side of the bridge and see whose stick will come out first.
- Race 'boats' down a creek.
- On a smooth reach of water, demonstrate your skill in playing ducks and drakes. Your child can look for flat stones for you, and be suitably impressed as you skim them across the water.
- Take a container and catch tadpoles or guppies to look at. They prefer to be put back before you go home. In parks and reserves, nothing must be taken from its habitat.
- Fish for freshwater crays (yabbies or marrons), especially in the warmer months. Tie fresh meat to a piece of string. When you feel a tug, pull it in slowly. Watch out for the nippers! If you want to keep the yabby for a few days, leave it in half an inch of water. If you cover it with water it will drown. Did you know that yabbies can flip themselves along backwards?

Rolling All Around

Some Boats to Make

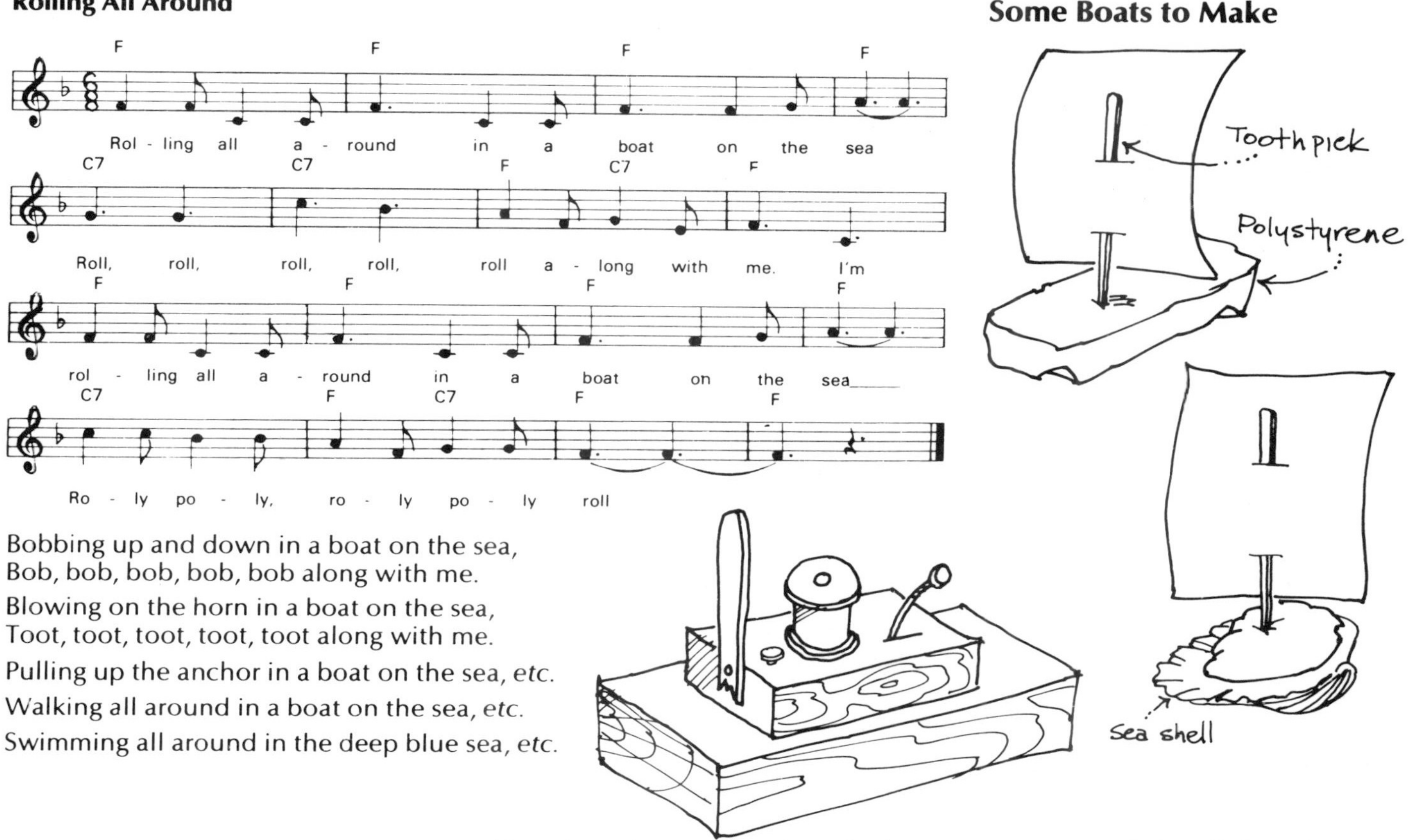

Bobbing up and down in a boat on the sea,
Bob, bob, bob, bob, bob along with me.
Blowing on the horn in a boat on the sea,
Toot, toot, toot, toot, toot along with me.
Pulling up the anchor in a boat on the sea, *etc.*
Walking all around in a boat on the sea, *etc.*
Swimming all around in the deep blue sea, *etc.*

If you're going to float them for long, use waterproof glue. Sail the boats on a baby pool, in the bath, or a bowl.

Two Little Boats

The boating rules for young children are the same as for adults:
Wear an approved lifejacket.
Keep the boat evenly balanced.
Don't overload the boat.
If the boat capsizes, stay with the boat.

EMERGENCIES

Telephone numbers

Keep these phone numbers handy:

- Emergency services ....
- Police ....
- Ambulance ....
- Fire ....
- Poisons Information Centre ....
- Your local doctor ....
- Your local hospital ....
- Your Children's Hospital ....

If an accident does occur in your home, which is your closest hospital casualty department?

Do you have a basic First Aid kit in your home?

All accidents are potentially dangerous. If your child is involved in one and appears to be unhurt, do watch him or her closely for a few hours.

Some Facts about Poisons

Every year in Australia thousands of children need medical attention as a result of poisoning accidents. The main groups of poisons are:

Medicines
Aspirin and other pain killers, iron tablets, heart tablets, sleeping pills and anti-depressants, antihistamines. Medicines are only safe when used by the person for whom they are prescribed.

Kerosene and petrol products
Kerosene, petrol, mineral turpentine, diesel oil, liquid furniture polish.

Caustics and corrosives
Drain cleaners, oven cleaners, caustic soda, acids, bleaches, detergents for dishwashing machines.

Pesticides and weed killers

What to do to Prevent Poisoning

- Never transfer medicine or any household or garden chemicals to a different container, especially not to a food or drink container.
- Keep all poisonous substances in a child-resistant cabinet.
- Dispose of all unwanted medicines by flushing them down the toilet.

In Case of Poisoning Accidents

Telephone
As soon as a poisoning accident occurs, always contact your doctor or Poisons Information Centre and identify the product.

First Aid
Keep Syrup of Ipecac handy, and if advised to give it follow the directions on the label carefully. (Syrup of Ipecac causes vomiting. It is available without a prescription. Next time you go to a chemist, buy a bottle to keep at home.)

There are some poisoning accidents where you must not try to cause vomiting, as the rising fumes will do more damage. These are:

- when the child becomes sleepy or unconscious
- when the child has swallowed a petrol or kerosene product, a caustic or corrosive. In these cases, give milk — it will absorb some of the poison.

Do not use salt and water to cause vomiting, as salt can be very dangerous in large amounts. If you don't have any Syrup of Ipecac, tickle the back of the throat with your finger.

Poisons Information Centres

Adelaide (08) 267 4999
Brisbane (07) 253 8233
Canberra (062) 43 2154
Darwin (089) 20 8385
Hobart (002) 38 8485
Melbourne (03) 345 5678
Perth (09) 381 1177
Sydney (02) 51 0466

Basic First Aid Kit for Home Treatment

- Antiseptic solution
- Antiseptic cream
- Syrup of Ipecac (50 or 100 ml). Get medical advice before use.
- Methylated spirits
- Calamine lotion
- Cotton wool
- Band-aids
- Gauze pads
- One or two simple bandages
- Scissors
- Fine tweezers

ANY ACCIDENTS BEYOND THIS TREATMENT REQUIRE MEDICAL ADVICE

Material for the above information has been supplied by the Child Safety Centre, Royal Alexandra Hospital for Children, PO Box 34, Camperdown, NSW, 2050. Phone (02) 51 0466.

SERVICES FOR CHILDREN

In each State there are many different organisations dealing with the care and welfare of children and their families, e.g. pre-school kindergartens, baby health centres, play groups, long-day care, family day care, before and after school care, parents' co-operatives, etc. The following organisations in each State should be able to direct you to the appropriate service for your requirements.

NSW
Department of Youth and Community Services,
(Advisory Section, Early Childhood Services)
323 Castlereagh Street,
Sydney 2000
(02) 217 7100

VICTORIA
Pre-School Child Development Branch,
OR
Maternal and Infant Health Branch,
Public Health Division,
Health Commission of Victoria,
555 Collins Street,
Melbourne 3001
(03) 616 7777

QUEENSLAND
Department of Children's Services,
(Early Childhood Resource Unit)
64 Mary Street,
Brisbane 4000
(07) 224 6333

WESTERN AUSTRALIA
Department for Community Welfare,
(Early Childhood Services Unit)
81 St Georges Terrace,
Perth 6000
(09) 321 0244

SOUTH AUSTRALIA
Department for Community Welfare,
Childhood Services,
GRE Building,
50 Grenfell Street,
Adelaide 5000
(08) 217 0461

TASMANIA
Child Care Unit,
Department of Social Welfare,
140 Macquarie Street,
Hobart 7000
(002) 30 8011

AUSTRALIAN CAPITAL TERRITORY
Department of Territories and Local Government,
(Welfare Branch)
PO Box 158,
Canberra 2601
(062) 46 2211

NORTHERN TERRITORY
Department of Community Development and Services,
Centrepoint,
The Mall,
Darwin 5790
(089) 82 1211

ABC PROGRAMS FOR CHILDREN

The ABC welcomes feedback from viewers and listeners. Makers of children's programs are particularly keen to receive comments because of the difficulty of pitching programs correctly at the level of the child's interests and understanding.

The ABC Education Department makes programs which are shown in school hours. It also makes programs for adults about child-related subjects, and programs for pre-school children.

If you'd like to comment on the programs, write to the ABC Education Department, Box 9994, GPO, in your capital city.

If you'd like to receive ABC Enterprises free colour catalogue, write to Freepost 230, ABC Post Box 10000, GPO, Sydney 2001. Phone (02) 437 9105 or (02) 437 8188. Telex AA176860 ABCENP.

ABC Products

Play School Program Notes and Schedules: Information about the songs, stories and activities in every *Play School* program, and the date on which it goes to air

Hickory Dickory: Songs from *Play School* and *Kindergarten* on LP record or cassette

Hey Diddle Diddle: Songs from *Play School* and *Kindergarten* on LP record or cassette

Humpty Dumpty: Songs from *Play School* and *Kindergarten* on LP record or cassette

Wiggerly Woo: Songs from *Play School* on record and cassette

Once Upon A Time: Stories from *Play School* and *Kindergarten* on LP or cassette

The Play School Picture Poster

The Play School Frieze: Pictures of Play School people and toys

The Play School Toy Posters: A set of 5 posters illustrating the Play School toys

The Play School Jigsaws of the toys Big Ted, Jemima, Hamble and Humpty

The Play School Yellow Book

The Play School Altogether Show, At The Zoo: Video cassette

About Children: A selection of 5 cassettes of talks from the radio series *About Children.*

Periodically new publications are added to this list. Further information may be obtained from the addresses above.

The A B C gratefully acknowledges the permission of the following to include copyright material in this book:

ALLANS MUSIC AUSTRALIA PTY. LTD. for *Everybody Do This* an American folk song with words by Mary Miller, *Here Is the Beehive* by Paula Fajan, *Eency Weency Spider, The Wheels Of the Bus* a German folk song adapted by Elsie Smith, *Where Is Thumbkin* from *Finger Play* by Mary Miller and Paula Fajan; for *Two Fat Gentlemen* and *Mr. Frog* from *Movement Songs and Singing Games* by Mary Champion de Crespigny; *Bathtime* and *If You're Happy And You Know It* by June Epstein from *A Day of Songs*; for *Fire Engine* by A Wiehard from *The Little Singers Song Book, Singing A Cowboy Song* by Margaret Denison and Margaret Fletcher; and for *Open, Shut Them* by Laura Pendleton MacCarteney, *Spot* by Arthur Herzog Jr, and *Pop Goes The Weasel* from *Songs For the Nursery School* by Laura Pendleton MacCarteney; for *Warm Kitty, Soft Kitty* an English folk tune with words by Edith Newlin from *Songs For the Nursery School* by Laura Pendleton MacCarteney and *This Little Boy* by Paula Fajan from *Finger Play*, all published by Allans Music (Aust.) Ltd.; and for *Here's A Ball For Baby* by Emilie Poulson published by J Curwen & Sons; LEEDS MUSIC PTY. LTD. for *When All The Cows Are Sleeping* by M Russell-Smith from *Wide Awake*; RON GAMACK for *I Am the King, Up and Down, I'd Like To Drive The Big Blue Bus*; SILVER BURDETT CO. for *Train Is A-Coming* by James S Tippett from *Making Music Your Own* Vol. 2; PRENTICE HALL for *Nicholas Ned* by Louise MacBride; CASTLE MUSIC PTY. LTD. for *One Potato, Two Potato* by Peter Charlton and Paul Read and *Build It Up* by Peter Charlton from *Bang On A Drum* published by the BBC and KPM; J ALBERT & SON PTY. LTD. for *Let's Go To The Zoo, All the Fish Are Swimming In the Water* and *Little Red Waggon* by Beatrice Landeck; PAXTON MUSIC LIMITED for *How Does a Caterpillar Go?* from *Physical Training Action Songs* by M C Dainton published by Novello; ROBIN MACKELLAR for *The Lion*; TOM FIELDING for *Stop, Look & Listen*; PETER COMBE for *I Can Run As Fast As You*; BOOSEY HAWKES (AUST) PTY. LTD. for *Five Little Candles* by Dorothy M Parr and for *Nursery Rhymes* from the *Oxford Nursery Song Book* published by Oxford University Press; MCINTOSH AND OTIS INC for *Sing Me* by Eugene Fern from *Birthday Presents* © 1967; ESSEX MUSIC GROUP for *Put Your Finger On Your Nose* and *Take You Riding* by Woody Guthrie and for *Jump, Jump, Jump* by Lionel Morton from *Bang On a Drum*; A & C BLACK for *I'm A Little Teapot* by Clarence Kelly and George H Sanders and for *Eat Brown Bread* by Gail Smart from *Okki-Tokki-Unga*; FABER & FABER for *Bananas in Pyjamas* by Carey Blyton from *Bananas in Pyjamas*; PETER CHARLTON for *The Elephant Wobbles*; PETER CHARLTON & PAUL READ for *One Day A Hand Went Walking* and *Zoom* GEORGE G HARRAP CO. LTD. for *Heads and Shoulders* by Linda Chesterman from *Music For The Nursery School*, and for *How Many People Live At Your House?* by L F Wood from *Singing Fun*; JEAN CHADWICK for *Three Jelly Fish*; SIMON & SCHUSTER, a division of GULF & WESTERN CORPORATION for *Fooba Wooba John* by Marie Winn & Allan Miller from *The Fireside Book of Children's Songs* by Marie Winn & Allan Miller; MICHAEL CAULFIELD for *Litterbug*; ANN NORTH & MARTIN WESLEY-SMITH for *Clap Your Hands, I'm Cross, Ring, Ring, I Feel Sick, I'm So Hungry, Squeaky Old Truck, What Will I Be Today,* and *I'm Hot (Running To the Corner)*; RICHARD CONNOLLY for *Play School*; JOHN FOX & WARREN CARR for *Here's A House* and *Spot Song*; VAL DONLON for *Put On Your New Shoes, Rolling All Around, Listen and Living in the City*; LIZ OLSEN for *Wet Washing*; JOHN FOX for *Here Is the Sea*; JENNIE MACKENZIE & ALLAN KENDALL for *Bubbles*; PETER COMBE for *Don't Forget Who You Are*; EVAN JONES for *Hey, Good Morning*; BELWIN MILLS for *Little Shell* from *The Small Singer* by Roberta McLaughlin and Lucille Wood, © 1969 by BOWMAR/NOBLE PUBLISHERS INC., Los Angeles, California. Copyright assigned to Belwin Mills 1981; BELWIN MILLS for *Fat Hippopotamus* from *Singing Fun* by Lucille Wood and Louise B Scott, © 1954 by BOWMAR/NOBLE PUBLISHERS INC., Los Angeles, California. Copyright assigned to BELWIN MILLS 1981; THOMAS Y CROWELL for *Jack In The Box from Another Singing Time: Songs For Nursery and School* by Satis N Coleman and Alice G Thorn, © 1937, Satis N Coleman and Alice G Thorn, renewed 1965 by Walter B Coleman, Dr Charles H Coleman, and Linton S Thorn, *A John Day Book*, and for lyrics and melody line from *The Animals Wake Up* and *Rain Song* from *Singing Time: Songs For Nursery and School* by Satis N Coleman and Alice G Thorn, © 1929, by Satis N Coleman and Alice G Thorn, renewed 1957 by Satis N Coleman and Horace E Thorn, *A John Day Book*; CURTIS BROWN for *What Shall We Do When We All Go Out* by Ruth Crawford Seeger from *American Folk Songs For Children*, © 1948 Ruth Crawford Seeger, renewed 1976 by Michael Seeger.